WE ARE THE SACRED FEMININE RISING

THIRTEEN WOMEN SHARE THEIR STORIES OF HEALING, TRANSFORMATION & RISING IN THEIR SACRED SERVICE

ALEXANDRA-JO HASTINGS   BROOKLYN VIENNEAU

CHARLOTTE SZIVAK   IDA HALLIDRI   OLIVIA DYDYNA

POLLYANNA BLANCO   RABIA SUBHANI   REVA WILD

SABRINA MABEL NICHOLSON   SACHA BRYCE

TANYA LEBLANC   TANYETTE COLÓN

VANESSA FERARRO   SANDRA RODRIGUEZ BICKNELL

SOULFULLY ALIGNED PUBLISHING

Credits:

Cover Art done by Parita @tailored.art

This book and its proceeds are dedicated to the Native Women's Association of Canada whose mission is to advocate for and inspire women and families of many Indigenous nations.

Thank you.

"They Tried To Bury Us, They Didn't Know We Were Seeds" - Mexican Proverb

CONTENTS

INTRODUCTION

The feminine collective has arisen and reclaimed their power. At a microcosmic level, these stories tell of deep wounds and struggles; challenges which are overcome with resilience and courage. Watch these amazing women as they tap into their inner strength, embrace their sacred Divine Feminine, and rise to healing wounded womanhood on a global level.

Follow thirteen resilient and diverse women as they share their personal life stories full of pain, love, heartbreak, and triumph. Through each chapter, you will hear how they navigated their life's voyage to cross an ocean of challenges to emerge triumphant, empowered, and ready to heal the world.

In this book you will learn the strategies these women used to help them cope with life challenges. You will walk the paths they walked of heartbreak and hear how they healed as they shared in the pain and power of their healed childhood wounds.

You will get to know how they stepped into their feminine power and embraced their Divine Sacred Feminine.

You will see through their eyes all that life has to offer when you can see past the hurt, the suffering they have overcome and use their wisdom to heal others.

Each chapter of this book has a different life lived, a different challenge, and a different resolution. These amazing women have carved out their own piece of lived history and used the knowledge and wisdom they gained along the way to share with their sisters. Their compassion and deep abiding love for humanity has led them to paths of healing in all fields and modalities. They are ready to serve and heal as warriors of light and love. The question is are you ready to receive?

Learn how to claim your right as a woman to overcome and rise like they did!

WHO IS WILD WOMAN?
She's the grit and grace inside
that insists you use your voice.
She's the inner howl, urging you back
to your wildish nature, demanding you
listen within and act without.
After a millennia of surviving a patriarchy
that would plunder the natural resources
of our inner and outer lives,
humanity has begun to cry out for the divine feminine.
And she is returning. Through you.
For there is no force more powerful
than a woman determined to rise.
~~~~~~~~~~~~~~~~~~~~~~~~~~~~~~~~

Poem by Angi Sullins

ALEXANDRA-JO HASTINGS

THE (GOOD) KARMA OF TRAUMA

his is the story of my pain and suffering in childhood, and how like many of you, it led me into darkness. An (almost) complete disconnect from my soul after a series of traumatic events, that lead to poor choices, that lead to breakdowns, that lead to deep healing when I was only 23.

I'll start the story, but just know, this isn't where it really starts. As you will find, our story never starts with us; and the things that seemingly "happen" to us in life are actually a guide to our most divine alignment—A healed and conscious version of ourselves with purpose and fulfillment.

I offer this story as a prayer; as a flicker of hope in the hearts of those who have been silenced, shamed, blamed, abandoned and hurt.

Underneath it all, there is light.

I was six, and it was the day of my mother's funeral. All I could do was feel and try to be strong in a way that I did not know how to be. I remember knowing very clearly what was going on and why everyone was gathered that day, yet, I felt calm. I already knew it was coming. I remember feeling a different kind of sorrow than what everyone else was displaying. It felt like they were grieving her loss, whereas I was heartbroken for her. It was at that moment I knew that it was not cancer that took her. It was something else, a feeling of hers that I could feel, too. I was six and I understood that an unseen darkness had taken her life.

I don't think my father knew what to do. In the years before my mother passed, he travelled for work to support her breast cancer treatments, so he wasn't around full time. Acting from his pain and love, things changed—fast. I had just lost my mother, and within months I had a new step-mother, three step-brothers, a new school, and was moved away from where I grew up and where a lot of my mothers' family was. My whole life flipped upside down. I no longer felt cared for or connected to anyone, and I felt like an alien with my step family. I had been taught manners, kindness, softness and good communication—and all these new people did was yell and scream. They were constantly fighting, even physically, and my step mother drank a lot.

It was a completely different environment and vibration.

Almost immediately, my eldest step brother began to condition and molest me, and no one was paying attention. Eventually this ended, and it was that rejection and lack of humanness in my own home that sprouted my deeply rooted narratives of unworthiness, activating the ancestral wounds of being a woman, as well as (as I would find out later in life), Indigenous.

Feeling silenced and forgotten, I wasn't a generally happy child after that. The same pain, suffering, and silence I felt in my mother had made a home in me. I worried a lot, and expressed deep fear of irrational things. I didn't tell anyone but more often than not I was in a constant space of heartbreak and anxiety. A fear of always being left. I desperately wanted to be liked and loved, but didn't know how to ask for it or receive it. Most of all, I did not feel worthy of it.

I stayed silent in this, continuing to disconnect from the people in my life when the plague that is suffering caught up with me again. Cancer had taken my childhood best friend, the only light in my life. When he got the diagnosis I remember knowing he wouldn't survive, and that I was meant to be his friend through that. Being there for him gave me purpose, and felt good in my heart.

That's the thing with darkness, you start to feel it coming before it's arrived. I began to have a cunning and accurate knowing of when bad things were about to happen— a trained eye — and in that familiarity, birthed the natural skill set needed to hold space for it. His death did something to me. It was as if it had hit an off switch. By the 9th grade I was so disconnected from my body, that patterns of anorexia, drinking, numbing, partying, self harm and mutilation had all crept into my life. After losing my virginity and having my heart broken by an older boy, things started to unravel.

The summer after this, it all resurfaced.

There I was, 15, but seven years old again—in the same loop, unable to cope with my emotions in a healthy way because I, like many of us, was never taught how. Unthinkably dark things that should never happen to any child had happened to me, I couldn't believe it. The memories so vivid in my mind, bubbled up from the pit of my stomach, like a firey ooze all over my body. I couldn't bear it, but couldn't speak it either.

And as if I had opened Pandora's box, not only was this the summer I really started to slip into drinking and smoking weed, but this was also the summer my life became a storyline straight out of a Jerry Springer show. A family life that consisted of cheating, lying, betrayal, projection, anger, shame, guilt and suffering. It was exhausting.

With these memories resurfaced, not knowing how to deal with the chaos of my life, and my addictions, I'm not surprised I slipped and took a visit to the psychiatric ward... for the first time.

By this point, partying and putting myself in unsafe situations had become my norm. I was at a party, and had drank way too much. I was alone in a tent with a older boy I thought liked me... the last thing I remembered was saying no and trying to push him off if me, but the next morning, in a very public and traumatizing way I learned that he had sex with me anyways.

I called my (now estranged) stepmother, hoping for some refuge, but I knew I couldn't tell her. Silence had now become a deep part of the pattern. I got home, locked myself in my room and broke down. My body was in shock, and my psyche had slipped into psychosis. I was a child crying out for her mother's love again. Convulsing and weeping. Eventually, my father kicked open the door, picked me up, and brought me to the hospital. I stayed there for a week, in that tiny gray room with that tiny square window, before I finally convinced him to sign me out. Though, I was never mad at him for doing that, he was doing the best with the information he had.

After that I had played with the idea of finally speaking out about what I had gone through. I remember knowing that it was doing something to me, like an infection oozing out into all corners of my life. I was mustering up the courage to tell, to ask for help but silence won, once again.

One fall Friday night just as I was about to go out with my friends, my father sat me down at the kitchen table to tell me that he had stomach cancer.

Here we go again.

The next few years of home life consisted of treatments, surgery's, chemo, radiation, juicing, hormonal mood swings, and arguments. And, in my teenage world, it was binge drinking on the weekends, promiscuity, and a secret addiction to stolen codeine.

My father died before my 18th birthday, and just like I had foreseen myself being an orphan in childhood (because remember, the trained eye), I was. This is where I really go off the deep end. Not long after my family doctor told me that I was suffering from severe PTSD, but I was so far from a place of healing that I couldn't even receive the fact that there was something significantly and noticeably wrong. And down that rabbit hole I went.

I lived in this loop of self harm and disconnection from my own soul for the next five years.

Partying.
Drugs.
Promiscuity.
Materialism.
Numbness.

Then, one morning, I woke up to just how much pain I was in.

I woke up hung over and had missed a meeting. In a panic I did what I always did when I was feeling almost any emotion at all—I reached for the little orange pills. As I leaned off of my bed to reach my home pharmacy shelf, I slipped. The whole thing went up, and came crashing back down on top of me and like a still frame from a very sad movie, there was a confetti of pills of all different shapes and sizes that stood still in a cloud around me. I was lucid, but time froze.

Then it hit me. I finally saw the shadow and chaos I was living in.

I realized that this was not my life.
I realized how confused and scared I was.
I realized how alone I had been feeling this whole time.
I realized that I couldn't put on the facade anymore.
I realized that I needed serious help.

My humility found me.

My heart was crying out for consciousness. The immediate awareness that something had taken over my mind was REAL. It felt like a curse, a dark spirit, something living in my mind that wasn't mine. This was my spiritual rock bottom, and because it was what I knew, I took the step and admitted myself to a very private mental health hospital for a PTSD inpatient program.

The first month of living in that facility was hard for me, and I was very resistant. I will admit, I was young and triggered so of course when I look back there could have been less ego, but there was still a sense of frustration due to a lack of resonance with the energy and environment.

The space did not feel supportive.
I felt like no one trusted me.
I constantly felt judged.

No one mentioned energy or sixth sense awareness.
No one mentioned visions or hearing voices.
No one mentioned Spirit.

...My primary way of experiencing life.

It was shame, pills, and control. They were taking me further away from how I wanted to heal. I didn't want to take medication to stop me from dreaming, or feeling. I wanted to go into the dream, and I wanted to rip open the feeling.

I searched for that missing piece in a nearby yoga studio that I walked to a few nights a week. And there, in the breath work, I found it. This is where I was finally still enough to find myself amidst all the noise. This inner voice felt so good to listen to, like it wasn't me, but this outside source—guiding me. Finally, the inner connection with Spirit that I had felt when I was young had returned.

I walked away knowing that it was all meant to be, but that this was not it for me.

I remembered what my father had taught me when I was young—to heal with the earth by playing in nature, talking to the stars, swimming in the lake and sitting by the fire. I knew there had to be another way. Another way to heal, another way to live, another way to love... and I was on a mission to find it.

This was my true commitment to healing, to Spirit.

This was when I knew my life was going to change, almost as if I had begun to play with the idea of giving up my "free will" to the light inside of me. The goodness.

An awakening of the heart.

Following the trail of yoga, not long after that I found myself on the beach in Thailand studying to get my 200h YTT. In this is a whole magical story of synchronicity, sisterhood, conscious community, movement, moon ceremonies... and LSD. It was the first time I experienced conscious healing through mind altering states. I remember it feeling so natural to me, like I had come home to the earth, a daughter of Gaia, finally. I felt grounded within myself in a community of people I FINALLY resonated with. People who had words and structures for what I was feeling so deeply my whole life, and healing modalities and tools that finally fit together with what I was missing. Like the perfect puzzle piece.

I knew in my heart that Mama Ayahuasca was calling. I knew I had to heal my heart with her. So, I got home from Thailand and bought a trip to Peru. I borrowed $900.00 from my best friend at 11pm that night. Even though the fire was lit, it took me five years to get there. That night when I purchased the trip, I heard the voice... a direct knowing that I was not yet in a place of preparation to meet Her, Ayahuasca, and that I needed to learn more about myself, and the universe.

And so, in a split second I made the decision to quit my job, looked up "spiritual schools Toronto" and enrolled full-time at the

Transformational Arts College to become a Holistic Health Practitioner. It literally happened just like that.

I was so excited to start class. Literally, a hop in my step and a pencil box of tabs and highlighters. I knew that I needed to continue my healing, but I wanted to be able to do it myself—to become my own healer. It was the first plunge into the dark ooze. Going through the spiritual modalities and holistic curriculum became a year of self therapy, Monday to Friday, 9 to 5.

I started to open my third eye and notice myself from the inside out, while learning how to treat myself emotionally, mentally, energetically and physically—with the earth and energy medicine. It was like having a blueprint to my soul, and an index on how to heal what blockage.

After this I went straight into service, offering lymphatic drainage massage and reiki in a shared therapy room in Kensington Market, the hippie hub of Toronto. I started hosting spiritual workshops and events all over the city, painting your aura, heart chakra ganja yoga, things like that... I was 27 and on the brink of my Saturn Return, and everything felt wrong. Exposure and opportunity was going to my head.

I knew I had to let it all go. So, I got rid of the healing room. I broke my contracts. I let go of my clients. I gave away my stuff, and moved to Costa Rica.

I moved to Costa Rica because I knew it was what my soul needed, I knew it was closed to medicines that would heal my ego, and really heal the darkness—the curse. I had never been there, didn't know anyone, had nothing to do, and no plan. I figured I would sit there until I got a sign.

And then, it happened. A sign.

I saw a post on Facebook advertising a half moon ceremony and even though I had never heard of it before, I knew it was the peyote. I knew there would be a fire. I knew there would be prayers. I knew there would be songs. I knew there would be my people there.

In a long flowy skirt I skipped around that fire like a little girl. I loved everything about it, somehow even though it was a completely new experience to me in this life...it all felt natural, and I knew what was going on—time stood still. That night reconnected me to prayer.

It was the start of everything.

I prayed for guidance, and alignment.
I said thank you, over and over again.
I vowed to live a life that reflected the medicine, and its teachings.

It was the activation that needed to happen within me, in order for my path to manifest. I had stepped into the world of Native American Wisdom and Shamanic Healing. I knew that this was the way I was going to live the rest of my life—that these ways of praying to the earth, connecting to all living things, all elements, great spirits, the water, the river, the birds... I was finally home. I finally let go of the darkness that wasn't mine. I found love, peace and harmony in my heart for all my pain, all my darkness.

I started to realize that BECAUSE I had been through so much, and had been to such deep dark depths within myself, I had the ability to hold space for others who had as well. The ability to feel their pain, and with all of the learned tools could also support them on their own healing journey.

Every little bit of pain and suffering has been relevant. My soul chose its trauma in an attempt to heal it in others on this planet. I know it is my soul journey to help others see their energetic, emotional and karmic narratives in their lives, past lives, and ancestry. How do I know? Because it is. It's as simple as that. When you heal yourself in this way, you never have to worry about "who you are" or "what you do" ever again, because when you make choices from the heart, and answer the call to help others, it happens organically. Your medicines and teachers present themselves. Your path presents itself, and you've done the work to reconnect with your soul, and intuition.

I would not be who I am today if it were not for my trauma. I would not care this much. I would not see what I see. I would not have the ability to stand in the face of darkness and evil. I would not have the fire in my heart to help others heal from their deepest pain—that thing that brings me the most joy in life. Every experience has taught me how to hold space for another soul who needed support and healing. Everything was divinely aligned and necessary for me to be who I am.

Whatever it is that hurts you most in life, whatever your deepest fear is...

I pray you find the courage and strength to face it.
Make it your friend.
Release it.
The darkness.
Feel your feelings.
Let out your anger.
Cry and sob into the earth.
Heal your inner child.
Look into the things that have been carried through the generations in your family.
Ask about your birth story.
Connect with your angels, spirits and guides.
Be vulnerable, raw and real.
Be forgiving, towards yourself, and others.
Notice the narratives.
Unlearn what you were taught about love, power, and goodness.
Reconcile.
Lay offerings.
Give yourself permission to let go of the guilt and shame over what you did or what you said.

Give yourself permission to let go of your anger towards those who hurt or wronged you.

Be free.

The darkness inside of you does not define you.
The darkness you have embodied is not yours.
It has been placed on your soul, like a plague.

Have the courage to heal it,
Your most magical life is waiting on the other side.

My dear brothers and sisters holding onto darkness,
I pray you find your way home, to Pachamama, and radical self love.

Aho,
All My Relations

ABOUT THE AUTHOR

ALEXANDRA-JO HASTINGS

Alexandra-Jo Hastings is an internationally known soul healer and life coach. Focusing on the soul of the inner child and ancestral karma, it has been joked that she is an "energetic death doula" as the death and rebirth cycle are a large part of her work. Also called "a multiple months-long ayahuasca ceremony," she holds space for others to open their darkness and heal their karmic wounding. She invites her clients into a safe space to talk about their trauma, to find the karma of it; and how to change it... After stepping into this path to heal herself, she now does it with the collective in mind as well. Studying deeply with plant medicines and her teachers, connecting her to her Canadian indigenous roots, as well as notable Spiritual Teacher Dr and Master Zhi Gang Sha. She is a tao hands practitioner and Tao soul communicator. Much of her work reflects shamanic beliefs, rituals, and teachings. Alex is a healer who teaches others how to be healers for themselves and the collective.

Instagram: https://www.instagram.com/sheisyourmedicine/?hl=en

Link tree: https://linktr.ee/alexandrajohastings

BROOKLYN VIENNEAU

MY BODY IS HOME: A RECLAMATION OF SAFETY, SOVEREIGNTY & ALIVENESS IN OUR SACRED VESSELS

*S*ince I can remember, my wild spirit has longed to find the meaning of home.

I was fortunate at a very early age to have discovered love in the form of ice dancing. During a horrific divorce between my parents, my mother and grandmother were committed to finding a space for me to blossom in and amongst the chaos of my family life. At the age of 2, I was introduced to the world of skating, and my ancient soul began discovering her glide. By age six, my coaches paired me with a young boy with whom I shared a love for creating art on ice, and together we went on to compete at an elite national and international level for eight years.

Skating felt like home. It was a creative outlet that was boundless in its ability to remove me from the breakdown of my family, challenge my limited understanding of the world and expand my capacity to know and trust my own inherent strength. It gave me a place to safely express my authentic nature. It offered me an entire universe of creative consciousness to explore. To me, skating felt like heaven on earth. When my young, developing mind couldn't fathom the themes of intergenerational trauma playing out in my family, skating was my place of solace. It saved me time and time again.

In many ways, I skipped over the innocence of being a wondrous child and was inserted into a paradigm where performance was my purpose. I woke up each morning with a deep devotion to a mission that required all of me in full presence, discipline, resilience, ferocious hunger, and unyielding volition.

While classified as a sport and athletic by nature, figure skating is subjectively judged and measured by image. Very early on in my life, I was programmed with the belief that in order to belong in the world, I needed to look, present, move, and be in a particular way. I became acutely aware of how my body looked, how I was being perceived and how I presented in relation to other teammates and competitors.

The programming was infused both subliminally and blatantly into the culture. On top of the already existing social pressures being projected onto young women to adhere to a standard of beauty, the world of figure skating was, like many other image-oriented sports, a breeding ground for disordered eating and self-image.

Rather than my body feeling like a vessel for creation, it was treated more like a machine that needed to meet specific requirements in order to function optimally. As my body began to mature, I noticed that I looked different than the girls I trained with. My shoulders were broader. Hips fuller. Thighs thicker. As my career with my skating partner progressed, the elements of our competitive programs suffered because it became more challenging for him to lift me. The realization that my body was outgrowing the standards of the sport was agonizing.

In one of our final seasons together, my partner and I were chosen for an international assignment in Mexico City. A national monitor visited our home rink to assess our programs and offer feedback. My skating partner was celebrated for his strength. I was pulled aside and told by this man that I needed to lose 10 pounds before we competed in Mexico. I don't remember how, but I lost the weight. I was 13.

I had been managing a severe back injury for years. My coaching team advised me to take some time off the ice to rehabilitate before what would have been a successful season. I remember being at my training site, in the gym facility with windows that overlooked the rink. I was watching my skating partner and my teammates practicing while on the elliptical. One of my coaches walked into the gym with his skates on, came over to my machine, and cranked up the intensity. "If you want to look like the other girls, you're going to have to go faster."

I didn't see it at the time because I was deeply conditioned for success at all costs, but the world of figure skating was inherently flawed. An outlet that was intended to support the expansion of my spirit contrarily served as a box to keep me small.

Somewhere along the way, my passion became clouded by politics and pressure. Skating became less about celebrating creativity and more about competing, comparing, and being the best.

My eight-year ice dancing journey ended against my will when I was 14. My coaching team ordered me to stop as my injury continued to progress. A world without skating was a world I didn't know how to exist in. I went from training several hours a day to being unable to get out of bed. I fell instantly into self-destruction. Eating myself into numbness and drinking myself into oblivion, I lost all sense of who I knew myself to be.

With the sudden and drastic shift in my lifestyle, naturally, my physical body began to change. The thing I was taught to fear and avoid most happened: I gained weight. And it happened quickly and uncontrollably.

I wandered recklessly through my adolescence, searching for anything to fill the empty void inside of me. I searched for home in anything that could dilute my suffering. I chugged bottles of vodka until I blacked out. I binged shamefully in private. I had disempowered sex with anyone who would give me even just a moment of recognition. Nearly every choice I made was a reaction to unresolved trauma, and a means to dissociate from the deep inner turmoil I felt being in my body.

I believe my weight gain was an accumulation of the denied, rejected, unmet aspects of my shadow looking for love and acknowledgement. Shame is a dense emotion. Grief is heavy, too. There is evidence to support the reality that the emotional baggage we carry often manifests as physical imbalance or dis-ease, and physical weight serves as a shield of armour to protect our deepest vulnerabilities.

When I was 18, a tragedy struck my family, and it shifted the trajectory and direction of my life radically. It awakened me to the humbling truth that I was spiralling into a vortex of darkness that would eventually become too impossible to return from. This acute trauma, while being the most unfathomably painful thing I'd ever lived through, offered me the opportunity to decide. To continue to submerge myself in destructive behaviour or to empower myself to choose life. Recovery. Healing. Transformation.

I chose to rise. The most obvious aspect of my life that I knew I could gain control over was my body. I began exercising for the first time since quitting skating and put myself on a restrictive fad diet. My body began responding to my efforts, and I got a taste of satisfaction for the first time in years. I was shrinking.

Losing weight felt like an intoxicating redemption, and I couldn't get enough of it. I was receiving praise from every direction, and it was giving me some semblance of hope that maybe I could feel at home in the world again. I wasn't actually resolving any of the dysregulation in my nervous system as a result of extreme trauma; weightloss was merely another means of escapism. Another manifestation of my disconnection from self.

Eventually, I landed on a decision to enter into a bodybuilding competition. I missed being in the spotlight and longed to perform again, especially now that I had something impressive to share: a perfect body. I trained vigorously for a year. Each bicep curl, fat burner, and pound lost was a step towards finally loving and accepting myself. I recall losing my period and feeling a sense of pride. My coaches congratulated me. "That means you're doing it right," they celebrated. A few weeks before competing, I ended up in the hospital in a state of severe depletion. I kept going. Forced. Pushed far beyond my body's safe threshold. All in the name of the comeback I desired.

I won the competition. I will never forget the full spectrum sensory experience of standing on that stage with my friends and family in the audience, a judging panel of white men sitting in front of me, a group of spray-tanned, equally as hungry women standing next to me, as I held this trophy in the air. Instinctively, I knew I'd win, but I imagined this moment feeling much different. Instead of feeling pride, completion and joy, I felt empty. I hadn't won anything; in fact, on top of losing more weight than my body naturally wanted, I lost my way. I lost my why. Memories flashed from nearly every season of my life where I'd felt so convinced that this moment here, this milestone of carving the perfect body, would bring me home to myself. And to my surprise, I felt further away from home than ever.

The anticlimax of my bodybuilding competition brought me into the trenches of my untapped darkness - again. After starving myself and eating a diet void of nourishment for months on end, my body held onto every morsel of food I fed it, and the pendulum swung from extreme weight loss to extreme weight gain. My body was changing at a rate that my mind couldn't begin to make sense of, and my attempt at controlling it was failing. Truth be told, my body reached an unsustainable and dangerous state of malnourishment, and it felt like it was fighting back, confused, trying to find its baseline—again.

I crumbled—physically, mentally, emotionally—into an experience of debilitating depression. For the first time ever, I listened to the cry of my body as she was begging for collapse. So, I quit my corporate job and offered myself the spaciousness to heal. I had no idea what that meant, but for the first time in my life, I honoured my intuition, and it felt hopeful.

This experience was familiar. There was a pattern repeating itself. The bodybuilding world mirrored the skating world in many ways, and this karmic theme came back around, full circle, back into my awareness, so that I could tend to the wound and heal it with tender compassion for myself and for humanity.

Now, I had enough of an understanding of myself to see that perhaps this breakdown was inviting me to break through into a paradigm of radical self-love. I had no idea what that meant, what would be required of me, but I desired it so desperately.

To find peace. To feel at home in my body. The experience of looking in the mirror had become nearly unbearable. I wished to crawl out of my skin and back into the version of my body that was smaller and seemingly more worthy of approval. I loathed taking up space. I could sense the judgment in people who witnessed me gaining weight, and it was mortifying.

"At least you're pretty."

"You'll get your body back someday."

"Have you tried keto?"

I was publicly harassed, blatantly shamed, and made fun of on the internet by a group of people in the fitness industry, too. That was fucking painful.

It penetrated my deepest core wounds. All of it. It revealed how unsafe I'd felt in my body since being a young, performative athlete and showed me how conditioned I was, along with the rest of society, with the notion that I ought to shrink myself in order to be loved and valued.

I went into hiding. I think I went three weeks without leaving my apartment or even my bed. For the first time in my life, I couldn't bury my pain. I had no option but to allow it. I cried uncontrollably for weeks on end. As powerless as I felt being cracked open, I knew it was leading me somewhere I'd never lived before: home.

I wrote in my journal every day for months:
My body does not define my worth. I love and accept myself exactly as I am.
My body does not define my worth. I love and accept myself exactly as I am.
My body does not define my worth. I love and accept myself exactly as I am.

I thought that maybe if I cast that spell enough times, I would begin to believe it.

In devoting myself to seeing beyond the corruption and deception of the systems trying to shrink me, I began to wonder if it really could be possible to exist without fighting against myself. I started sensing that being in a human body was a precious gift and that we're all here for a purpose far greater than what I could see through the veil I'd been wearing.

I woke up. I had the quintessential experience of an awakening led by an intelligence that I was equal parts confused and captivated by. I could see and sense that I had boundless processing and dismantling and rebuilding and reorienting ahead of me, and I felt ready for the work because a whisper from the Universe told me that freedom was not only on the other side, it was here now.

I spent years dancing between paradigms. On the one hand, I was lifting the veil on the programming all around me, receiving evidence that I am the creatress of my reality, receiving confirmation through synchronicity, and seeing the world through a lens of colour for the first time. On the other hand, I was coming face to face with the truth that I had spent my life manipulating my body as a means of distracting myself from the trauma that lived there. It was time to heal. For me. For my ancestors. For all women.

I knew that my journey with body shame, disordered eating, and addiction to filling the empty void was an experience that carried resonance amongst many, if not all women. To some degree, we've all been convinced that we'd be better, more successful, more liked, more wanted, more accepted if we crunched ourselves into the tirelessly unrealistic beauty standards that infiltrate our perception of reality everywhere we walk. I knew I was not the only one. Upon the discovery that there was more to life than shrinking myself, I also discovered that I had a mission to serve; a movement to participate in; an initiation into freedom to lead.

After leaving my corporate job and entering into the unknown abyss of limitless possibility of the existential curiosity of "what the fuck am I here for?" my intuition guided me to become a personal trainer. I desired to show people that they could love the experience of reclaiming their health without having to punish themselves with fitness and food. I was still coming to terms with my own body and healing my relationship with movement, food, pleasure, and sexuality. Still I knew I could help people discover their own strength in a way that was unconventional and unique, so I leaned into this fiery passion growing in my womb.

As I remained steadfast and devoted to my own inner work, I noticed that the deeper I travelled into understanding my core emotional wounds and survival patterns, resolving the trauma from my past, connecting with divine intelligence, and disentangling myself from the matrix of diet culture, the more my physical body reached homeostasis and balanced itself naturally. I had been so brainwashed by the systemic body image narrative that calorie deficits, and intermittent fasting, and squats on squats on squats would help to regulate my confused body, but something groundbreaking happened. When I surrendered the need to fix, control or change anything, and redirected my energy and awareness to feeling my feelings, my body began to heal itself.

The paradox is that as soon as I stopped trying to change my body, my body changed. And not in the way that I was attached to. She changed on her terms. She softened and surrendered. My body knew what she was doing all along, and all I needed to do was trust her.

This is what I learned: we can unlock the key to wholeness and healing by observing our relationship with everything from our past. When we free stuck energy in our bodies, process old trauma, create presence around parts of our shadow who are crying for us to listen, our bodies re-establish their power and lead us as they were designed to.

My life's work then became full-spectrum. I was not a personal trainer; I was a transformational leader—a freedom facilitator. A walking, talking, dancing permission slip to show others that nothing needs to change in order for them to embody raw, hot, untamed self-honour.

Presently, I don't have a physical home. I answer the call of my intuition and move nomadically from place to place, meeting new parts of myself and cultivating deep roots and sensual sanctuary everywhere I walk.

My soul's mission has evolved as rapidly and potently as I have. Though I wish the treacherous storm of body shame on no human, it happens, and knowing that my story holds the wisdom to support women in returning home to themselves, I understand why it happened to me. For me. For us. My heroine's journey is your heroine's journey. We are all wild warriors walking with shields through a tempest of ancestral hurt and societal expectation and impossible beauty standards and pressure to conform, and I'm here to walk with you in and through the storm, in and through the body and in and through a radicalizing pilgrimage to a land of sovereignty. You're closer than you imagine. In fact, what if I told you that you could arrive now? How would it feel for you to remove the armour, strip yourself bare and let the storm drench you in liberation?

It is with ferocious passion and heart that I lead women to remember who they are. As a transformational coach and healer, I support women in many corners of our earth to restore their relationship with themselves, be freed from the trauma of their past, reclaim their sensual nature and discover incredible joy through honest self-expression. I hold deep reverence for those who walk courageously and curiously into the exploration of their human experience and it is my honour to hold the space for real, full-bodied transformation to occur on a physical, emotional, spiritual and energetic level.

Our bodies are not trophies. Our bodies—they are homes. With lush gardens of wildflowers. With windows to the sun, the moon, and the galactic unknown. With structures painted in colour and decorated with beauty. We can rebuild, rearrange time and time again. And when we decide it's time to strip it all down, the foundation remains: Our minds of brilliance. Our hearts of strength. Our wombs of creation. Our cells that dance in divine harmony with the soul purpose of breathing life into the earth. Our bodies will hold us through many seasons, and for as long as we're here, no matter where we wander, we're home.

May we undomesticate ourselves from the rules placed on us by institutions operating from fear, for we need not be afraid of our own power. May we release ourselves from the shackles of a culture designed to separate us from our true nature. May we nourish our sacred vessels with soul food that activates delicious, sensory pleasure, and may we assimilate it all as medicine.

We are multidimensionally powerful beings. We can awaken our Kundalini, open our third eye, manifest abundance through the frequency of orgasm, complete karmic cycles from incarnated timelines, work with the healing power of crystals, communicate through universal light language, receive messages from spirit guides, channel alien starseeds... And in my experience, feeling safe, sovereign, at home, and alive in our human bodies is the most radical expression of spirituality there is.

Every stretchmark on my hips tells a story of reclamation. The way my stomach jiggles as I dance creates ripples of invitation for the feminine to shake freely. The size of my legs reflects the strength of my spirit walking on earth. Each time my body expands in preparation for a bleed, I embody the rhythmic nature of the moon. My body, she is home.

I invite you to celebrate the warrior strength of the vessel that carries you. To witness your reflection through a lens of Love and to see what Love sees. To say "I see you. I honour you. I love you." again, and again, and again.

All of you is holy.

Your body does not define your worth.

Your body, she is home.

ABOUT THE AUTHOR

BROOKLYN VIENNEAU

Brooklyn Vienneau is a Transformation Coach and Energy Alchemist who empowers women to feel safe, sovereign and alive in their bodies. With roots in emotional embodiment and shadow integration, her work safely and intentionally guides women to meet the parts of themselves who have been rejected and abandoned through the experiences of trauma throughout their lives, and leads them into the remembrance of their wholeness. Through private mentorship, group coaching and events, Brooklyn's gentle and honest approach to communication and teaching serves as a portal for her clients to transform their health, wealth, relationships, purpose and sense of self.

Website: www.brooklynvienneau.com

Instagram: @Brooklyn.vienneau

CHARLOTTE SZIVAK

UNLEASHED: YOU ARE THE SACRED SITE

"*P*sst -hey! Look down" I could hear the voice but yet, "'Aloha, Ohana!!! Oye!! Look down!" This was now a demand.

To my surprise, as I peered downward, there amongst the beach was a rock in the shape of an outstretched hand glistening in the bright morning Sun. As I reached for the stone, I could hear the whisper of the most beautiful melodic voice singing, "You will always be guided."

Cue the magickal Hawaiian rainbow and the Whale pod breaching, dancing amongst the waves, gifting us with a magnificent tail flip - I was left speechless, my jaw dropped, as tears rolled down my cheeks and my Lightbody tingled all over.

A defining moment.

We have but a few in our lives, those instant realizations, the A-ha moments of absolute certainty, like a lightning bolt gifting us with a glimpse of the future path -moments of collapsing into the Divine Alchemy that is held within the fusion of empty presence and adoration between the connection of absolute ecstasy and surrender.

From that moment on, I further committed myself in absolute service to the divine, humanity, this solar ring, and Gaia, further surrendered my body, mind, and soul to be an instrument for the Divine God/dess. Even though I was already breaking the mould, from what I was taught I should want or be; not wanting to have a 9 to 5, ' stable job', get married, and have the 2.5 kids—I kept things low key, shrinking wherever possible, not setting my life on fire, walking on eggshells not to upset anyone, explode, or expose my truest self; that wild, unbridled, magickal, living light emanation of joy, sensuality, enLIGHTenment, and devotion just fizzled. This lackluster spark was brough about from what seemed like endless scolding and criticism, and after a childhood of sexual abuse, narcissism and hurt, losing myself in spirituality was my way to survive.

It was easy to become an overachiever, my life began to read like a list of accomplishments; media personality, behind the radio station microphone, Tarot card reader, cheerleader for over 30,000 brave soul clients, groundbreaking radio show producer and host of 'Goddess Alchemy and Divine Magic', psychic consultant to the television and Hollywood movie industry; Multi-Sensory conscious event leader; online Healing Vortex Queen for other leading spiritual/business influencers and programs; keynote speaker at thousands of engagements; newspaper celebrity; guest and advisor to many shows on Global TV, SLICE, CTV, USA, Discovery, ELLE Canada, REUTERS; the Official Psychic for 10+ years on the #1 rated Morning Radio Show Y108FM and later on the Iconic 102.1 The EdgeFM in Toronto; I was honored to be interviewed by 100's of radio shows globally, including being at the 90th Academy Awards in 2018; and appearing in a few Hollywood blockbusters over the years such as, "How to lose a guy in 10 days", "The Pacifier" and "Hairspray".

PHEW!!

As if that wasn't enough I poured myself into the role of fundraiser for Breast cancer research for 5 years. This led to being nominated for Distinct Woman of the Year 4X's in Health and Wellness and

Community Leadership. Did I feel satisfied or fulfilled? No really. I was honored to be recognized but I still felt I had to play it small, it was a fear of igniting persecution, shame or outshining anyone. I was actually a very shy, sensitive person, but give me a passionate topic and I lit up. I felt unworthy but driven, so I overcompensated.

It was easy to carry the role of award-winning psychic workaholic. I would introduce myself as having over 6,000 years of past life experience. I trailblazed the profession for 15 years across North America on tours, doing 1:1 mentorships, LIVE events, and 12 years of leading sojourns to Sacred Site Retreats.

In my off hours, I would continually invest tens of thousands of dollars in myself. Always healing the next level, especially shadow work, accelerating my vibrational frequency, connecting with my etheric teachers, the Starseed councils alchemical healing sessions, clearing the ancestral genetic lineage, diving deep into the akasha; clearing the past, present, and future parallel timelines. Activating ley line grids, portals, and anchoring cities of light while igniting the temple of light globally, leaving charged crystals in waterfalls and blessing the water. Taking shamanic training, various courses, books, anything and everything that quenched my soul's thirst to heal thyself, balance my karma and be able to deliver innovative, cutting edge healing modalities. I became a soul-full business strategy sage, was introduced to vibrational alignments and essences, while also received ongoing Venusian Temple Rose priestess path initiations, ceremonies, rituals, and activations to remain relevant, fresh, and always elevating for all my beloved soul and animal clients.

And they came in droves. They were always seeking, searching when all else had failed. They craved connection. They have been to all the healing courses, psychics, yoga retreats, Burning Man, read the books, and still couldn't figure it out. They just knew that something was still M I S S I N G. They wanted something different. Depth. They came from all walks of life; some were successful AF uber rockstars, teachers, CEOs, start-ups, baristas, politicians, students, doctors, authors, royalty, officials, or actors, and still, something just felt OFF. They all wanted to get L I T from within.

I was perpetually so stuck in the doing, the male side of my abilities, that I forgot how to Be. But the shining presence of my luminescent Goddess energy betrayed me. My sparkling eyes deceived me, the stillness and enchantment my soul finally began feeling gravitated outwards in waves to the many that chose me to connect them to their essence, soul guidance, and gifts. Unbeknownst to me, awakening them in an alchemical shift from their greatest pain to the infinite possibilities, the as yet undiscovered horizons their souls were ready to ignite and fire up.

They all knew the truth, the truth I somehow still hadn't figured out or accepted about myself yet.

That I was an unfurling power of nature, and the elements combined, a cosmic Stargate awakening the holy of holies by stepping into the throne of my inner sovereign Queen-dom. A portal to enLIGHTenment, a wild wombmxn who was a Soul Healer divine channel and a High Priestess of the Kundalini Serpent flame Sisterhood who shared an all-embracing view of spiritualism that helped tie the shimmer threads together of the ancient-future timelines of truth, power, and wisdom. A soul she/her that was here to help guide them home reconnecting them with their Source.

Just before the great pause of 2020, I was satisfied but getting more restless with my path of touring in the exact same locations, lifting the vibration one city at a time, and meditation events without fail every two weeks for 13 years. It felt like a never-ending psychic hamster wheel, and I was exhausted from an unknown race against time. I felt stuck. I had climbed so many mountains but had forgotten to celebrate the view. I wished to infuse more playfulness and pleasure into my life. I was craving more of the Goddess energy, the Divine Mother, (sure I had shimmering glimpses at a few pivotal moments in my life) but the spirals of awakening energy made my womb cry out in pain. I needed deep rest, nurturing and craved the feminine flow approach to life with creativity, and art. How could I become more receptive, juicy and sensual?

Then on Samhain (Hallowe'en) 2019, in an unexpected ending, the universe stepped in and reminded me once again it was time to surrender and allow my path to expand further, one luminous step at a time. Isis, the Queen of Heaven, Empress of the Stars herself, appeared before me. She was reminding me, "The time had arrived to call all the priestesses back to the temple." I was overjoyed at the thought of being reunited once again with her and my sisterhood. It brought back the remembrance of Isis's words from decades past - when I would escape into my vivid dreams of lives past from Egypt, Lemuria, and Avalon. Instantly the veil she placed upon my third eye dissolved, and my visions filled with sparkling pyramids, the most intoxicating scents of plumeria, and rose gardens surrounded by white columns, and lions lounging around the temple pools under the shimmering rays of the moon and night stars.

As a young teen, I had become so obsessed with Egypt that I could read and translate the hieroglyphics. That was until the night the Divine Mother Isis appeared and requested I stop losing myself in the past and get grounded in my present incarnation. She also spoke of what was to come of the future timelines "when she would return to ignite all other Priestesses, Goddesses and Queen souls in preparation for the Reawakening and Rise of the Divine Feminine". Immediately feeling a veil being placed over me, protecting the sacred knowledge, I quickly forgot about Egypt and dove into my life.

For the next few years, nothing really made any sense; what I felt, the light beings, and animals I could communicate with - I thought everyone could do this. What was so special about it? I felt heavy, draining energies filter through my body. My hands poured out limitless energy and symbols. I had no idea what it all meant. I started seeing colours and holograms around people filled with fire letters, light-beings; even their organs and tissues would reveal their own intelligences of geometric shapes, glyphs, and codes. It was as if I had X-ray vision. Since there were no words to express what was happening, I remained silent.

I started seeking out magick, having no idea what I was looking for, just that I would recognize it by how it felt. Which then drew me to waterfalls and nature. I always seemed to be surrounded by trees, lakes, and rivers. Wisps of wings, hearing a faint voice, or seeing light out of the corner of my eye, as I'm sure many of you have also experienced. One morning on a gorgeous waterfall hike, three light beings came down to greet me wearing the most stunning iridescent sapphire blue robes of light, introducing themselves as the Pleiadian Emissaries of Light, and gifted me with a single pink rose.

Then from every night onwards, I would soul travel to their star-system as they taught various KA/ BA healing activations, Cosmic, Earth, and Body Kundalini transmissions infused within their chambers and temples of light during my dream states. Then in my waking hours, I began integrating all this cosmic wisdom and transmissions with my existing abilities and practised creating more magick that I could then give in all my offerings of Lightbody healing sessions, divine guidance - soul readings, or meditations. I even co-creating Holographic Journeys to Egypt as Khemet slowly started creeping back into my awareness. Eventually, the Sirians, Arcturians and Galactic Federation joined in, further continuing my healing training practise which eventually led me to become an Oracle with Full Sensory Perception.

After experiencing a Shamanic death rite a few weeks after Samhain, a circle of priestesses appeared surrounding me cloaked in the silkiest of black satin robes reflecting the shimmering Milky Way and night sky. I instantly recognized her presence, her indescribable energy brought me to my knees in reverence. It had been decades since our first encounter during a kundalini yoga meditation. There stood the Magdalene shimmering before me, holding a black rose that she placed lovingly within my heart chamber.

Mary Magdalene shared with me that it was now time to awaken a mystery school collective that would re-activate the cellular memory embedded from within our blood, bones & DNA. Igniting our souls to remember the universal cycles and rhythms spiraling from and within she/her, the cosmic consciousness of the womb rose grail path for this solar ring sparking all who identify with her/she in reclaiming their sovereign, sacred and holy selves.

A holographic image of the Venusian pentagram then lit up before me, and Mary Magdalene said that since Venus would guide the journeys as she was about to begin her next eight-year sky dance. It was crucial I stepped into the true role I was born to be. This was what the Star nations had been preparing me for since that fateful waterfall hike day.

Within the depths of my soul, even with the limited tech knowledge I had, it was clearly time to launch and transcend into this new stratosphere. I just had no clue how it would all come to pass. I was on a tight schedule with clients and mentorships about to embark on a cross Canada 16 -city tour. So I surrender and let thy will be done.

The first lockdown was an absolute shock.

As the world recoiled from fear and bewilderment, I took my first breath and stepped into a new terrain that actually terrified me— Facebook LIVE. No longer hiding behind my past accomplishments, I brought back my radio show, 'Goddess Alchemy Divine Magic' rebirthing as the Goddess Alchemy Collective Mystery School Oasis and took that plunge—the fear and chaos were enormous as I, myself, was reeling from a cancelled five-month tour that excited me to no end. It was time to pivot. Ironically the first day I went LIVE was also the day Saturn moved into Aquarius, signifying work evolution with electronics, and online tech! I dove in and did one of the most dynamic transmissions on clearing the Fear Matrix I ever had the luck to record (Available on my Youtube channel- https://youtu.be/ 5ZBReiHcB3o). The first half of the pandemic kept me laser-focused, creating a powerful mentorship container within Goddess Alchemy that blew open my interstellar abilities and awakened the embodied transcendence of my clients. With multiple gathering transmissions that aligned souls across the globe. I was speechless with all who chose to show up. The path was lit by the sky dance of Venus, unlocked by her rites, of ascent and descent. Joined by Isis, the Magdalene, and Queen's council chamber all co-creating the initiatory gateways of the legacy of the ancient womb grail codes of the sacred rose of Sophia-Magdalene, the feminine Christ consciousness. We birthed the Sovereign Rose Womb Queen, a 13 moon spiral, and my signature program with an option for a coronation pilgrimage to Egypt.

Divinely designed, we began on the September Equinox, celebrating the changing of the seasons, marveling at the natural flow of the Goddess Wheel of the Year with the pulsating rhythm of the Inner Womb Medicine cross. I became fully absorbed within this new path as we entered the Royal road of the Yoni towards the Holy Womb Temple. We began dissolving thousands of years of trauma, sexual wounding, trust issues, powerfully witnessing each priestess, and healing aligned with the Lunar Keys and celestial star knowledge. Without the pandemic, I would never have been able to create any of this. I couldn't believe I was so lucky to be able to truly devote myself —I was filled with so much utter gratitude to every woman that entrusted me with her soul as we traversed into these magical realms.

The second lockdown shattered me.

I felt limited and collapsed into the abyss of no-nothingness. Because I had quarantined alone the entire time, feeling like no one needed me, who would I be if I didn't sacrifice or martyr myself to be the savior? I had an identity crisis. Being so used to rushing in during a crisis to help take on transmuting my clients' pain, I never noticed till it was too late that I developed a massive fibroid, my clenched jaw, or how high functioning anxiety stress I was managing until my health was in distress. The hunger to keep working, elevating my vibrational frequency, take on more shadow work, and keep bettering myself was gone. In her place was this ferial woman with a curious expression. Sure I still wanted to travel and work with my beloved clients, but in a different way, a more balanced way. How could I always support my clients but not give this to myself?

Lockdown number two changed everything.

I began to uncoil myself, rescheduling appointments for a few weeks to literally sit in silence within absolute darkness except for a few Moroccan lanterns lit, cocooning myself as if I had been planted. Deep rest is not idle, not wasteful. I kept reciting to myself, rewiring my thoughts with affirmations realizing how sometimes rest was the most productive thing you could give yourself and your body. It was a new feeling for me. I felt supported, not having to prove or tame myself to fit into a box of what a psychic should look like or be.

The Hathors, Isis, The Black Madonna, Mary Magdalene, Lilith, Yeshua, and the Black Ray all guided me to soul travel to the Venusian Etheric Temple. They invited me to lie on a rainbow moonstone crystal slab for healing as they weaved through my dormant, distorted, and divine aspects. I completely surrendered and let them do as they wished. Afterward, I felt swaddled like a newborn baby allowing the magic of their alchemical adjustments and actualizing the energy fluctuations of the crystalline frequencies within my soul, consciousness, and body.

My own soul metamorphosis and transfiguration at the deepest levels enabled a clearer direct connection with Gaia, the cosmos, the elemental realms, and the forces of nature. It paved the way to confront my shadow of pain, grief with men in love and relationships, to truly embrace hearing the words of my inner masculine. My cellular changes were materializing into the very fabric of my core foundation reality. The peace I felt was indescribable. I relished the low hum pulse the earth was emitting and with the delicious sweet surrender allowed the Black Ray to filter through my etheric body. The Black Ray initiated a deeper state of purification, as this ray holds the alchemical resources of the Void, {the pure potential of infinite possibilities before they are birthed or co-created with the White Ray its polarity} and its finer particles of anti-matter supporting shifts into a higher reality.

I finally looked deeply into my own eyes, repeating affirmations learning to accept, forgive and fall in love with myself and my magnificence through the miracle of mirror work, and finally, for the first time ever, I read all the over

5,000 testimonials I had received from the precious souls I had worked with over the years. I was overcome with the gratitude and love I felt.

The pandemic and lockdowns were crucial for my soul's well-being. It actually UNLEASHED the radiance of my inner illuminance core, my own divine soul shined through, and suddenly the cosmic puzzle pieces fell together. They ignited new cosmic living light codes as they moved beyond doorways into magical dimensions further opened for exploration, awakening the sacred network of passageways within. I began realizing how my own organs, tissues, and molecules were the reflection of the sacred pathway meridians align to the cosmic web of creation, the ley lines of the elemental dragons, and the rose stargates of Gaia, My cells aligned with the orbits of the planets, and stars within this solar ring, Interstellar, living light transmissions alchemical tantrika goddess was born.

The ancient sirens of magic reawakened, taking full authority and sovereignty

Both grounded and yet connected in freedom to the otherworldly dimensions - the realm of Heaven on Earth. It was me all along. I was the Sacred Site I had been always searching for.

ABOUT THE AUTHOR

CHARLOTTE SZIVAK

An award-winning Oracle of Destiny, Charlotte Szivak is a Galactic Soul Alchemist, Quantum Healer, Spiritual Ascension Mentor, Founder of The Goddess Alchemy Collective. She was born on a New Moon Solar Eclipse, gifting her X-Ray vision and full sensory perception. A Visionary, Charlotte has appeared on numerous international TV and radio shows,

including CTV, Global TV, USA, & Discovery. The Official Psychic on Y108FM 'Mornings and featured in ELLE Canada, REUTERS, and Yahoo! Charlotte expertly guides thousands of global souls to complete alignment with their vision, inner sacred union, and the priestess path by awakening their brilliance, elevating their embodiment, gifts, and divinity with online sacred programs, retreats 1:1, and living light transmission offerings.

A Portal to Enlightenment:
www.charlotteszivak.com

Instagram:
www.instagram.com/iamcharlotteszivak
Goddess Alchemy Collective Facebook:
https://www.facebook.com/groups/345067175612724
Youtube:
https://www.youtube.com/c/CharlotteSzivak/videos
Living Light DNA Galactic Transmission
Sophia-Magdalene; The Sovereign Rose Womb Queen, 13 Moon Spiral
www.charlotteszivak.com/sophiamagdalenestar

IDA HALLIDRI

THE UNFAIRYTALE

I. THE PARADOX

I sat at my barren desk with just my computer and an unfilled application.

It was a sunny Sunday at the tail-end of November. The glimmer of the sun on the lake was deceptively inviting, only to deliver a sobering slap across my face if lingered outside too long, precisely as you would imagine cold Muskoka sunny November days to feel.

The room was filled with haphazardly packed things and a graveyard of memories. Every item that belonged to me, thrown together in unlabeled bins and boxes and bags. My unpacking nightmare.

In the short spurt of adrenaline that followed the crushing news, I had managed to erase every trace of my being from the place we called home together. I was almost upset at how little time it took, of how little of me truly belonged here. Though at this moment, I felt great gratitude for the part of myself which kept me moving before the crippling terror set in. The relationship was over.

I began to fill out the application,

> *"The yearning in my heart has always pulled me towards the understanding of our inner worlds. My fascination lies in dissecting relational patterns within and without. I have been on a quest to quench the thirst for understanding why so many of us, no matter how self-aware or successful, when it comes to relationality, we all face challenges that can feel immobilizing. The nature of love and the constant uncertainty that shadows it has been my muse."*

Feeling victorious after that last line, I paused to feel grateful at the significance of all of this. My foundation had completely vanished below me, and this training was the flotsam that was going to bring me back to shore.

I have wanted to go down the psychotherapy world route since I gave myself permission a few years ago to consider what I might enjoy pursuing outside of the confinements of what my dad wanted me to do. In an attempt to put words around many complicated feelings, I became fascinated by the world of psychology, psychotherapy, healing, and true transformation.

I tried pursuing two other graduate programs and was left feeling unfulfilled because of the pathologizing nature of most psychotherapy disciples and the co-dependent nature of healing to the psychotherapist.

I knew in my heart that Internal Family Systems (IFS) was going to be different. It didn't believe in things such as eating disorders or addictive disorders or any disorder for that matter because it was rooted in the foundation that we are all made of a multitude of personalities that *always* serve a benevolent purpose.

These parts that make up our internal family learned their behaviours somewhere along the way where it made the best sense for survival but might no longer be what is most serving right now. Healing—actual, real, sustainable healing, happens when these parts are witnessed in their pain and met with compassion. Not by some psychotherapist, by our own inner innate healing entity that exists unharmed, albeit sometimes dormant, inside all of us—what IFS calls the Self, for obvious reasons.

At this particular moment, you can imagine, I was very excited about this type of healing being a real possibility.

I continued to write,

> *"All other areas of our life have gone through tremendous innovation, but our relational awareness is, sometimes, still archaic in its conditioning. I always imagined I would need to have a thriving relationship in order to begin to speak about this, but I am now holding the understanding that a "failed" relationship is just as worthy of being a space for teaching with many possibilities for deep healing."*

In those last few hours at the cottage, I had to give myself purpose, and this was giving me purpose. I was making my mess, my message, as they say. Any semblance of meaning was necessary to continue to keep that crippling fear at bay.

I felt accomplished and closed my computer. It was almost time to go.

We took one last walk on the land, as Tim called it. The land was as vast as it sounds, at least in Toronto real estate terms. We were on a small lake called Saint John, which was more like a very large pond. It got warm in the summer, and that, my friend, is no Canadian lake.

The cottage was on a peninsula that stretched out into the water, offering a nearly 360-degree view of the shoreline. We sat on the rocks, held each other, and cried. Finally laying down the protective armour that kept us distant before.

Something really interesting happens at the bedside of death. We strip ourselves of all the protective mechanisms that played some role in keeping us safe, and we lay barren our souls.

This gave us both a great sense of peace. Love was there, and the only thing in the way was the protective parts that played some role in keeping us safe.

It's an odd feeling, falling in love while breaking up.
It's as bittersweet as it sounds.

The multiplicity of our existence can only best be captured and described with the paradox. Every single moment is an ending and a beginning. A mini funeral and a tiny birth paint each passing moment. The loss of everything that came before it and the promise of everything that is yet to come.

II. DISILLUSIONMENT

As early as I can remember, I imagined my life to be a fairytale.
My conditioning as a little girl is not unique.

I would gather all my dolls and play alone in my room. Closing the door behind me, I would claim whatever little privacy I could have at that age. Driven by little rebellions to do what I knew was not allowed, I played out little love stories with my dolls. Suzana was my favourite doll because she felt like flesh, and her knees would bend. She had long blonde hair that no matter how much came out in my attempt to brush it, she still had a head full of it. She was special because she came from Japan from my dad's work travels, and before her, dolls were stiff and hollow, but she had substance; she was real.

Suzana would always find herself in some sort of great distress, and precisely at the right time, she would be rescued by a prince. He would be represented by a less than ideal prince figure of a stuffed smurf or something of that kind because Ken dolls were too inappropriate for little girls. With the help of my excellent imagination, the prince would come and rescue Suzana from her woes, and they would fall in love and kiss while I made sure to keep my eyes locked on the door.

I have few memories from my childhood, but this one is very clear in my mind. Significant somehow, and yet, it is not unique.

My conditioning as a little girl is not unique.

I grew up in Albania, a small forgotten country in Europe. When I spoke about it, I received responses like "You're Albino?" and "Are you from Alabama?"

I loved my childhood the way children love what is familiar because they do not know better.

My dad was a hard man, in the way that most Eastern European fathers of little girls are. He was harsh and strict. A man of little words, he used terror to rein his household. He made the rules, and you followed them. He said so, and it was so. Having been the only one of seven kids to leave where he came from—a small village on the top of a literal mountain where cars cannot get to and donkeys are a high-class mode of transportation — he was tough on education and handed discipline more readily than smiles. He didn't really hit us, my older brother and I, except for sometimes when the atmosphere of terror wasn't enough to keep us in line. He went to the city, married my mom, and gave his everything to creating for his kids the life he never had.

My dad was a hard man, hardened by the pain of losing his wife too soon. I did not know it then, but he wore the silence of her passing like a cast over his broken heart. We all did, my brother, my dad, and I. We never spoke about it. Too young to make it all make sense and too obedient and terrified to speak up, I stayed silent. But I know now that it is precisely when lips shut that there is much to be said.

The little memories that I have of my mom feel like snippets from a movie that I watched a long time ago. They feel distant and like they do not belong to me.

Diana, a princess, always dressed in her nighttime gown, laying on her bed throne. I didn't mind this because this way, I could get a better look at her face. She didn't get up much, only to go to the bathroom or to yell at devious little girls that I played hairdresser with. She liked to comb my hair, a little bob with bangs, that disappeared when she disappeared. Significant somehow. I didn't have girl hair for almost a decade after that.

The terribly glitchy movie of my mom concludes with her laying in her bed in a room full of people dressed in all black, crying. Already mourning her. It was a regular day for me. I visited her in the room full of people dressed in all black and went by her side. I told her she looked pretty, and off I went again. Too preoccupied with five year old things like the cool watch on my arm, rather than the room full of people dressed in all black. I didn't see her again.

I didn't think much of it, I don't think. I don't remember. Repression is a helluva drug.

Our lives went on, and my family continued to collect silent things.

It wasn't as much the complete cut-off from the feminine example in my life that was hard. It was more so the heartless one that followed it. My dad remarried.

Either I was too sensitive, or she was too careless, but I didn't get the mother I had hoped for. I did get a younger brother though, who was my favourite toy and source of love. We had a lot of fun when Toni was born. I would host fashion shows, and he would be my model. My older brother was the cameraman, and these films still exist in European VHS tapes collecting dust.

We practically raised each other, Toni and I, those first years after we moved to Canada. He was four, and I was thirteen. He became my confidant, my partner in crime, my *alibi*. Since I was never allowed to go out, and my parents were working jobs like waitressing and pizza delivery in order to adjust to life in a new country where none of their experience or education meant anything, I had to spend the entirety of my time babysitting him. We did everything together after school, which I looked forward to way more than school.

I was an immigrant pre-pubescent-wanna-be-girl of questionable gender with a lazy eye. I sported short hair because I didn't have the sovereignty or courage to decide my hairstyle. I wore the same clothes multiple days in a row because of neglect and lack of know-how, having only worn uniforms before. To top it all off, I spoke, thankfully at least, only Oxford textbook English, not the cool-kids English. I only stuck out just a bit more than the other grade 8s.

I survived grade 8 the same way I survived the following decade at that home. I became malleable on command. I started living two completely separate lives.

My dad became an even harder man, the way most immigrant Eastern European fathers of adolescent girls are when they move to North America. Until I "finished" university, I was only allowed out if I conjured up a believable enough lie of going to the "library" or "studying with friends." Finished is in quotation marks because my longest, but not greatest, con was pretending I graduated from the University of Toronto in four years instead of the eight that it took me, the last four being secretly and part time. My greatest con, however, was pretending I still worked at IBM for over a year after I was laid off. This one took investment, financially and emotionally. I pretended to go to work every single morning before 8am and returned back home in the evening after a day's adventure filled with my favourite addictions—cigarettes, fast food, and Netflix, or whatever we called it at that time.

I had a credit line I opened once I heard I was fired, a car, and full unquestioned freedom, yet I felt completely imprisoned.

I was miserable.
I hated that home.

The pain of being constantly rejected by the feminine and unprotected by the masculine got so great, and so too did my emotional suppressants of choice until I finally gained the courage to dig up one silent thing that was rotting away my insides. In a moment of defeat, as I declared I was moving out, in not so many words, my dad confirmed that I was not crazy. That he had tried to get her to love me.

Moving out, I thought I was finally going to be free, but I was still trapped in the shadow cast by my conditioning.

III. THE JOURNEY HOME

My search for home was deeply woven into my quest for a fairytale. It was incessant and constant.

Yet as I look down the playground of my past, it's filled only with disillusionment.

Tim came into my life very unassuming.

He felt comfortable, genuine, safe. He was interesting and interested and never felt phased by my erratic outbursts. He said things like "that's great" when I spoke unspeakable things, and for the first time, my silent parts got a voice.

It was salvation manifest.
Our love story was slow to build and quick to fall apart.

It's usually tough to pinpoint when a relationship breaks, but for me, the moment is vivid.

It was the summer solstice, the longest day of the year, and it truly felt that way. We were standing on the deck looking out into the water like we often did at the cottage, but this day I felt my heart break. He'd laid down his vulnerable paradoxes that, in my eyes, only served to threaten the relationship. There was absolutely no space for his truths to exist if we were to maintain the integrity of the relationship. The illusion, rather. A gaping crack started to form, and a stream of doubt started to fill it.

The saviour had fallen short.
It was war after that.

I outsourced all of my love from him, and when he cut me off - because he had other things to do with his life like, you know, a job— my entire system was in danger. And when there is danger, we protect. I put on my favourite armours; I attacked, withdrew, and collected silent things. And he put on his; he shut down.

I outsourced all my security from him. I had demanded, in not so many words, he be financially responsible for me. At least I acted like it. I moved into his space and relinquished all of my responsibility onto him. All the while maintaining a peculiar rebellion towards him. It was a "don't tell me what to do, but please tell me what to do" scenario.

He had become a surrogate father.

I was a hard woman. Hardened by the absence of soft nurturance and the constant betrayal of attempting to outsource it. I had buried my mother and everything that she signified and was terrified at the prospect of being responsible for my own life. I still needed someone to tell me what was so.

Tim tried to communicate these things in his best, flawed ways, but I wouldn't listen. His truths only served to threaten the relationship, and having been unconsciously sourcing my most basic needs from him, there was absolutely no space for any of that. Thankfully he had the courage to put an end to it.

Something really interesting happens at the bedside of death. We strip ourselves of all the protective mechanisms that played some role in keeping us safe, and we finally listen.

The unrequited love story here was the one between me and my silenced parts.

I was ready to listen.

In an act of mini rebellion, or perhaps it was courage, I decided to travel to Mexico, during a world pandemic I might add, and only come back once I had "figured myself out."

The truth is I still am in Mexico, and I have found more than just myself.

In fact, I have discovered an entire village within.

With little skill and practice, but tons of heart and incentive, I started to close my eyes and listen inside. My flotsam came and with it a beacon of light into the dark, unfamiliar, turbulent waters of my inner psyche.

The core teachings of my IFS training gave me a map to step inside my inner little world. As I learned to become a witness to the very many different players inside, I grew curious. Giving the benefit of the doubt to the most dubious of characters, I began to get to know every single one that came knocking on my door.

IV. THE UNFAIRYTALE

We're told, "love yourself" yet we play favourites with which aspect of our self we deem appropriate to love and which we choose to villainize instead.

Certain aspects of ourselves, adored. Other parts, ignored.

We celebrate discipline yet punish chaos.
We toast to successes and mourn failures in private.
We strive for perfection and then exile overindulgence.
We revel at the sight of birth and fall silent at the bedside of death.

Every time we praise one aspect of our being and then disprove of another, we are declaring war inside of ourselves. It should come as no surprise that it is also precisely here that we collect our greatest wounds and most potent life treasures.

Something incredible happens when we meet our demons, not to abolish them, but to greet them with kindness, approach them with curiosity and get to know them and their story. They take off their protective armour, lay down their heavy burdens, and reveal the innocent, hurt, forgotten, silenced children that they have so tirelessly and valiantly been defending.

We search endlessly "out there" for our saviour, and we may find him for some time. We crave salvation from the other because we are so starved inside. Healing - actual, real, sustainable healing, happens when *all* parts of us are witnessed in their stories and met with compassion, not by some external saviour, but by our own inner innate healing entity that exists unharmed within all of us.

In the wake of disillusionment, I was forcefully nudged to rewrite the story I imposed onto my poor Suzana, just as it was onto me. I had been promised freedom and unconditional love, but all I saw was the shadow of my conditioning. The freedom I sought came in my sovereign ability to truly be with myself, all of myself, in all my parts. When I finally learned to listen and respond to my own inner demands in the way I fantasized my prince would, my conditioning started to collapse.

I began to write my Unfairytale.
Suzana saves herself in this one.

The path less walked, and majorly less attractive thanks to our collective subscription to conditioned gender roles, towards courageous love and lasting intimacy is through being in a truly committed relationship with ourselves. Through becoming the primary caregiver that we failed to get from mother and father, lost love, and outgrown romance.

The real love story here is the one between you and all your parts.

It begins with you being the one to warmly welcome the pieces of you that were once banished.
To give voice to the ones that were once silenced.
It grows with you learning to accept all of your unacceptable bits.
To validate internally what you seek externally.

And it builds with you being in the right relationship with yourself, giving soft nurturance and care to all of your inner world characters, especially when they least deserve it.

This is a cultivated practice of giving reverence to all of your seemingly negative and maladaptive behaviours and seeing them for what they truly are, self-preserving and protective. Not evil, not bad, just worthy and in desperate need of your love and attention.

Though this work is internal, you don't have to do it alone. The dark, unfamiliar, turbulent waters of your inner world are best journeyed through with the guidance of someone unafraid to uncover their own. What I offer is a space for self-exploration, with techniques to deepen your relationship to your innate Self-energy and your parts. Think of me as the flotsam gently holding you as your Self steers you back home.

If my Unfairytale has taught me anything, it's that freedom is on the other side of loving our unlovable parts. And let me tell you, it ain't no happily ever after. Instead, it's the whole damn spectrum of our chaotically complex and vibrantly rich expressions of our being.

ABOUT THE AUTHOR

IDA HALLIDRI

A delicious cocktail made up of equal parts storytelling, relational awareness, and inner world systems, always partial to the aesthetics.

With a background in digital marketing, copywriting, and design, Ida has always been driven by a good love story, even if it was between consumer and product. She answered to her inner yearning in 2021, when she became certified as an Internal Family Systems Practitioner, a psychotherapeutic modality that powerfully transforms our world within and without. She is a student, first, and a gentle guide to others, second, who wish to deepen their journey inward and insource love, compassion, and healing; what Ida calls the real love story.

Instagram: https://www.instagram.com/prettythoughts.ca/

OLIVIA DYDYNA

IN TUNE AND TURNED ON: A GIRL'S SEARCH FOR ORGASM

*W*hat if I told you your humanness is the key to your awakening and ability to experience higher states of pleasure in love and life? Through a journey of making the unseen seen, I was able to release blocks preventing me from experiencing sexual fulfilment. I am here to show you that sex and healing doesn't have to be so serious. When you embrace curiosity, building trust with your body will feel less like work and more like play. This unconditional trust in yourself will be the ultimate expander of your capacity to love. I will show you how to flirt with life and make love to the Universe, but first, let me tell you about how I got intimate with myself on a level beyond anything I could have imagined.

Quarantine happened, and I was secretly rejoicing. I got to work from home and finally take a break from the 9 to 5 office grind. Excitement filled me as I had all this free time to dabble in tarot readings, social media videos about galactic beings, manifestation tools, the power of la luna, fairies, sex magick, and all things ethereal. The amount of knowledge on the internet both excited and frightened me. The limit did not exist. Disappointed by the constant rollercoaster in my love life and career, this was my time to finally figure out my gifts so that I could pivot into a career that truly didn't feel like work and attract the man of my dreams. So I wrote out qualities of my dream job and partner in my journal, called upon the moon, lit that paper up, and got serious about making my life magical as fuck.

POOF

And this is the part where I tell you I woke up the next day, and it all came true, right? Well, not exactly - it was a pretty long ride with some dips and turns, but I was strapped in, and it was too late to turn back.

Let's first focus on the love part since it's more fun. I was the epitome of Anna Billier's *The Love Witch*[1]—("a modern-day witch that uses spells and magic to get men to fall in love with her, with deadly consequences.") Okay, so the consequences weren't so deadly, but they did pinch my heart a bit - or theirs. Miami was my playground as I'd dance until the morning and frequent many after-parties. I was an expert at finding club love, but the thing about club love, once you sober up, it tends to disappear.

The lust spell I had these lovers under only left me feeling dissatisfied once the sun came up. The fire I had during the chase quickly extinguished once in the bedroom. I never felt turned on when it came to sex. I wanted to connect on an intimate level with these lovers only to realize they were emotionally unavailable. I was attracting men with big bright red flags that I thought perhaps were some sparkly love-potential signs. Don't get me wrong, there were a few times that I attracted a great guy only to push him away. When they showed too much emotion, EW. On the other end, not receiving enough attention bored me. I was pointing the finger at these men that were not pleasing me in the bedroom. I was fed up and finally made a promise to myself —NO MORE BAD SEX.

I needed a shift, and lucky me, a fellow mermaid reached out about starting a love circle. A meet-up where we could dive deep into our love addictions to remove blocks that were preventing us from attracting (and keeping) that soul-gasmic partner. The four of us all had different patterns when it came to love. I was a master at flirting and getting the guy to sleep with me, but attracting a partner that wasn't toxic was a bit more complex. My friend called me out. "So you're unhappy with work and your love life. Would you be into a guy who also felt that way?" *Nope.* If I was to attract a partner in a high vibe state, I had to be living it. The work needed to start with me. I was hitting a wall. How was I to attract a partner if I didn't know what I wanted?

What do I want exactly? *blank stare*

If I don't know what I want, let's start with the basics: Who the fuck am I?

It was time to let go of Tinkerbell, who only thrives on attention and short term gains. It was time to get intimate - with myself.

The love circle was a safe space for us to share our personal experiences of love. We not only explored our upbringing and its effects on our idea of love, but we also used the circle to experience different types of healing techniques. Once a week we met and took turns hosting our meet-up. It was my turn to lead the circle and I wanted to experiment with psyciliban. This sisterhood felt like the perfect environment to utilize plant medicine for healing. Our intention was to experience more magic in our lives. With that in mind, I did my due diligence and did my research on Reddit for the proper amount to take to blast off. Slight disclaimer, we *probably* should have had one person take a little less, but that thought popped in after the fact. Once again, there was no turning back, and it was time to ride it out.

Our journey began with giggles and fun and then got a bit interesting. At the peak of the trip, I had to go to the bathroom as it was my time of the month, and if you've ever experienced the "bathroom dimension" I was in it. As I was going to the bathroom, I noticed I had bled through my pants. All of a sudden, I started seeing blood everywhere. Was I losing too much blood? Did I need to go to the hospital? Am I okay? I became so self-conscious in the bathroom and started worrying about getting my friend's apartment dirty, let alone causing an even bigger scene. I couldn't take it anymore and ended up shouting a faint cry "Heyyy…"

My friend peered in as I was sitting on the toilet with just my top on, covering myself awkwardly. "Is everything okay?" She asked.

"I don't know. Is this okay? Am I okay? Is it bad?" I wasn't sure. My hesitation and actions made my friend question if I wanted her to be there or not, but she could see that nothing major was happening.

As things were taking a long time, my other two friends were curious to see what was happening. At this point, all three of my friends were staring at me, asking me questions and doing their best to comfort me while I was half naked.

"Ohh, It's fine. It's just your period. It's natural. It happens once a month. I'll give you some pants."

We were all together in the bathroom and there was no judgment. There was no shame. This was nature.

The moment brought us closer together, and we felt such genuine love for each other after this experience. There wasn't blood everywhere as I realized it was my mind that created this scene. All was well, but I definitely had some processing to do.

Why did I go into such a shameful and confused state? In the moment, it didn't seem like there was any clarity on what happened, but the effects took place on a deeper level. Something had shifted.

It was the first time I realized I had a fear of being fully seen.

While I was able to get naked with men, I was never able to show my vulnerability with my partners. While I thought I was open to the world having fun and being free, I was not open to seeing the darkest parts of myself.

I always thought I was doing the work by externally seeking knowledge, going to every workshop, and being well versed in all healing modalities. What I didn't understand was that the work involved me facing my emotions—those feelings of loneliness, sadness, and unworthiness that I ran away from. Not only facing them, but holding myself with compassion in these emotional states. How was a conscious partner going to hold space for me if I wasn't able to hold space for myself? The hard truth was that I was, in fact, the emotionally unavailable one. I had to let go of the search for outside love as it was my distraction and escape from doing *my work.*

As I looked into the mirror, I was never able to notice myself but was so keen on seeing the other. It was through the eyes of the other that I began to learn so much about myself. The "Who am I?" question kept lingering.

While I was good at connecting with people and getting to know them, I didn't know myself. I was in a constant search to know what gifts I had or if I even had any. I made a commitment to discover my gifts during this quarantine, and my search continued. Through this search, I stumbled upon systemic constellation work and the power of the mirror.

Systemic Constellation Work, also known as Family Constellation, is an experiential method that uses energy embodiment to make issues and solutions visible. Imagine choosing strangers to role play so that you can get an outside perspective. What's fascinating is that the person participating usually has some sort of connection to the topic being discussed, so in turn, they also receive clarity and healing doing this practice. I began to participate in Family Constellation workshops, which pushed me to practice getting in touch with the energy of others and my body and how to get comfortable voicing the first words that come to mind. I began to experience how powerful group gatherings can be to make the unseen seen. These sessions helped me become comfortable working through family and personal issues in the presence of others and allowed me to practice vulnerability in front of strangers. I wanted all my friends to experience this and was eager to share my learnings and test it out with them. I wanted them to see how easy, fun, and healing it is. The opportunity came up, and I took the initiative.

It was a full moon, and a few friends and I were enjoying a walk along the beach. Since I love all things witchy, I suggested a healing circle. We sat down facing each other and began taking turns speaking out loud our intention for the circle. Next, we took turns choosing one person to represent our "problem" and one to represent our "solution". I was chosen as the "problem" where I had to embody the energy of my friend's problem and provide a message. As I was still new to this, I was a little nervous. It was my turn now, and all eyes were on me.

All of a sudden, a cry that was pushing to be set free surfaced forcefully. I felt such a heavy sadness in my heart as I was releasing the emotion. My friends and I were confused as to what was happening. At that moment, I didn't understand what I was feeling or experiencing, but for the first time, I knew this sadness wasn't mine. This experience was so intense it left me questioning what happened and what it meant. What were these feelings trying to tell me? Was I just projecting my own emotions and feelings? Was it really not my own? I was still trying to uncover the truth, and serendipitously a few weeks later, a friend sent me a podcast on Human Design.

Human Design is a system of learning about yourself and pulls in knowledge from astrology, I Ching, Kabbalah, and the Chakras. It seems pretty cool, right? I decided to look up my chart.

There it was. The answer that dissolved all the questioning and confusion I had about myself and my experiences. I was a reflector.

Reflectors are able to sample others' energy and mirror, absorb or magnify it. This finally explained what was happening to me. A friend once told me, "Isn't it funny how the mirror never sees itself?" It was the deepest truth I ever heard which made me realize why it was so hard to see myself and understand who I was. I am me, I am you. I'm able to show you parts of yourself and share the wisdom your emotions want to voice. My ability to express emotions allows you to see the strength in vulnerability and the transformative power emotion has. Your emotions do not make you weak. They allow you to fully experience your humanness and expand to feel even more profound states of pleasure and love. And then it dawned on me. In order to attract the expansive love I wanted, I too needed to expand.

In order to feel the profound states of love that I was seeking, I had to experience the full spectrum of emotions. This meant that if I wanted to feel multi-orgasmic pleasure, I had to release any fear of experiencing shame and sadness. Sexuality was the bridge between my body and soul. While I was searching externally for better and deeper orgasms, I was unable to fully feel the pleasure in my body. So what was preventing me from orgasming with a partner?

I would say I was a professional at self-pleasure as I started humping corners at quite a young age. As I became an adult, I never had issues with orgasm solo, but I had a massive block when orgasming with a partner. I was on a mission to figure out why my body would shut down or not be turned on. Being turned on and wet was so fleeting. I thought that if I just met the right partner, that would be the key to opening me up and turning me on. While I knew how to please myself intuitively, I had to learn what my body liked with the presence of someone else.

I started to experiment with meditation and breathwork to really get to know my body so that I could tell my partners what I liked. One night I decided to sit on my meditation pillow and play around with my breath to see if I could feel something switch on in my body. I put on a sacral chakra hertz meditation with headphones in and began to just listen to the sound of the hertz. With a hand on my heart, I started taking in big belly breaths through my mouth and began to guide myself with my mind. Something was telling me to breathe in and hold the breath while squeezing my sexual organs for a few seconds, and then release. I did this for about ten rounds, and all of a sudden, I started to notice a buzzing down below. The energy was so intense I started to get curious. I reached down and realized my vulva was vibrating and wet. I was shocked. No porn, no sexual thoughts even, just simply moving energy through breath with focus. I continued the breathwork and became more and more turned on as I was amazed by how powerful my body was. I didn't even care about the orgasm and was consumed by these new sensations. This was a window to the possibility of having ecstatic states of pleasure. I finally figured it out.

My turn on was never about the partner I was with; it was *me*. My body is the one that has the power to say yes or no. I was liberated. It was no longer about finding the perfect partner or the dream lover to feel states of pleasure and love. I held the key to my turn on and no one else. And with that, the responsibility was on me to create the conditions needed for my body to safely release. There was still one other thing to get curious about. Why didn't I feel safe with partners?

While this is a more complex question, I did know from my studies that women store a lot of trauma in their womb and vagina. Just like a tense muscle, it won't feel good unless the tension is released. I continued exploring and decided to search for a womb meditation on social media to do some healing. I found a beautiful shamanic meditation and followed where the music took me. After 30 minutes, something happened, I went into a childhood memory. I got flashes of moments where I was made fun of for masturbating by my parents and siblings. I started releasing a buried sob. I began to process those moments and see how they affect me today. As a small child, I didn't understand what I was doing, but all I knew is that it felt good. I started to connect that this good feeling was shameful, and I shouldn't allow anyone to see me doing this. Another lightbulb went off.

I was afraid to be fully seen by my partners and be shamed in my orgasmic state. Orgasm is such a vulnerable state, and my emotional body was preventing me from experiencing freedom and openness in the presence of the other. My body turned off to protect me from experiencing shame and abandonment. I yearned for connection with people so much that I couldn't risk being rejected. I chose my partner's pleasure over my own. I chose connection with the other instead of connection with myself. My obsession with sex and the orgasm was because I was yearning to feel connected, yet I learned I wanted to feel connected to myself.

With this shift, I began to choose myself in my partnerships and focus on my pleasure. Being truly seen by my partners became easier as I faced and accepted feelings of shame, guilt, and rejection, knowing that I would always hold myself no matter what the situation. It was trust in myself and my body that cultivated this ability to experience more turn-on and orgasms. I was tuned in to what I wanted, which in turn, turned me on.

To my surprise, as I began to choose myself in love, I was pushed to choose myself professionally as well. It was my time to choose what I wanted to do instead of assisting others with their dreams just to feel love and connection. I dove even further into sex, love, and relationship coaching by enrolling in Layla Martin's Vital and Integrated Tantric Approach Program. I wanted everyone to experience the magic of healing and empowerment that can happen quickly and with ease when you are open to it.

While things were business as usual at my corporate job, there was a calmness as I was less emotionally affected by stressful situations. It was my two-year mark as the Director of Customer Success, and I was called in by my CEO & CMO for a meeting. "Thank you for everything, Olivia. This was a hard decision, but the business direction is changing, and we no longer need your role." They were dissolving my role, and I was let go. Isn't it funny how the Universe sometimes decides for you? Stepping into my power and being turned on by life is a continuous evolution, but it starts with an intention to create a life that you are excited about. I finally learned what "doing the work" really means, and it's now my mission to help others on their journey.

Your emotions are here to teach you. Listen to them. Listen to your body. By no longer resisting my emotions, I am in a state of flow. I no longer focus on the end goal, but I am experiencing the joy of being surprised by the journey. My life is less serious and more meaningful. I experience orgasms with partners, but it's no longer my focus. There's less pressure and more play. And the beauty is that the expansion continues, and the possibilities are limitless. This is the gift that I want to share with you. By working with me, I will show you how to listen to what your body needs to fully open up and feel safe. Through breathwork and energy healing, I will activate your sexual energy so that you can experience the power of your creation. With my healing modalities, I will show you that doing "the work" doesn't have to be so hard or take so much time. I am here to hold space for you to be vulnerable so that we can bring to light the blocks preventing you from achieving your desires in sex, love, and relationships. I am seen.

Are you ready to be seen?

If you're ready to take the next step on your sexual evolution, reach out to me at olivia@besexessful.com or via Instagram @prettygypsydreams.

---

1. https://www.imdb.com/title/tt3908142/

ABOUT THE AUTHOR

OLIVIA DYDYNA

Olivia has always been curious about the human experience and has never shied away from talking about sex. Her approach to spirituality and healing is through playful exploration, and her methods include energy embodiment, inner child work, and sacred sexuality. With a background in sex, love, and relationship coaching rooted in the VITA method, she empowers women to experience a deeper connection with themselves and the world around them. If you're ready to be turned on by life, connect with Olivia.

Email: olivia@besexessful.com
Website: www.besexessful.com
Instagram: @prettygypsydreams
Facebook: https://www.facebook.com/olivia.dydyna/
Linkedin: https://www.linkedin.com/in/oliviadydyna/

POLLYANNA BLANCO

SO YOUR "YES" DOESN'T LEAVE YOU STRESSED - LET YOUR SACRED FEMININE GUIDE YOU HOME TO YOURSELF BY BALANCING YOUR CHAKRAS

*A*s women, we share a deep desire to serve others by giving our gifts to the world. Our hearts call us to make the lives of those around us better, and we want to make a lasting difference. Along the way, our intention to leave a legacy of love can end up leaving us empty, exhausted, and stressed. You are a beautiful creative feminine soul. If you feel like you've been barely treading water while you wait for someone to give you the same abundant love and care back, then from my heart to yours, I wrote this for you.

I don't want you to keep waiting indefinitely for 'The One' who will be there for you, see you, and hear you in all the toe-curling ways that your soul craves. For every night that you lie awake ruminating about your day and planning the next overscheduled one, for every promise you are honoring for someone else and every promise you are breaking with yourself, for every ounce of energy that you are lavishing on your loved ones and every moment you are longing for some downtime—left feeling lonely and left-out—I beg you to please stop! Breathe! And slow down.

I know from experience how jammed into the deepest darkest crevices of our psyche doubt lurks. For me, the question humming in the background was, "After all I've given to others, if something happens to me, who will look after me?"

So often, when we are highly driven in the outer world, it can be easy to dismiss self-care as frivolous, being mere cucumber slices on our eyes. Oh, how that pales in comparison to our impassioned drive to do-do-do and tackle the world's problems. There's no time for self-care, right?! What the divine feminine wants you to know is that slowing down, getting grounded, being centered in your heart, showing up with presence, setting healthy boundaries, practicing spiritual hygiene, listening to your inner guidance, embracing your shadow and light, cultivating an intimate relationship with yourself, restoring the sacred to everyday life is about becoming emotionally, mentally, physically, soulfully, and spiritually available to yourself—now that deserves a purple heart.

As I committed to slow down and calm down, it got easier to hear my higher guidance through all the noise. For so long, the unhealed masculine energy in me thought I needed to fix a part of me that was broken so that I could get on with things. Now the awakened divine feminine in me welcomes my wholeness, seeing all my experiences as life-giving sacred offerings to create from.

True self-care is a deep dive. As you learn to equalize your past experiences, your soul is invited into a sacred union partnership with your body, as well as your heart, mind, and spirit. It's about lovingly gathering all the bits and pieces of you that got scattered and ignored along the way when your ego-personality ran the show to keep you safe. As your nervous system relaxes, you can align with greater balance and harmony, and your inner masculine's wounds will heal in the loving presence of your divine feminine, restoring his divinity too. Just as a gorgeous butterfly-to-be transforms within her cocoon, I was transformed through the pain of hiding in my 'comfort zone' into the awareness there was truly nothing to do battle with.

The more of you there is to love, the more energetic resources you will have. Self-care relaxes the grip stress has on our body, and conscious chakra-care relaxes the grip our level of consciousness has on our whole being. As Einstein clarified, you cannot solve a problem at the same level of consciousness that it was created. So as our consciousness expands, those parts of us once discarded as 'junk' are now reclaimed as long-lost treasures. This sacred union process is this deeper self-care that makes everything else possible, and it's anything but indulgent. It's responsible. As much as I enjoy an escapist Hallmark movie, the 'One' you've been truly seeking is not outside of you—it's you.

This chapter will help you reclaim the power of your "Yes" and own it without apology. It will give you permission to value self-care so you can serve from an overflowing cup. And the self-care I'm about to share with you that transformed my life is not your typical go for a mani-pedi to unwind on a Saturday afternoon (as much as I enjoy that too). The kind of self-care I want to share with you is a soulful, sometimes messy, deeply enlivening, clarifying, and inspiring, techno-color inner awakening journey that will guide you back home to your true self. There's nothing fluffy bunny about it. Life gives us exactly what our soul needs to come home to deeper self-acceptance of our divine worth, love, and purpose. My heartfelt wish for you is that you may emerge through the stressful experiences in your own life, not bitter but better.

I sincerely hope my story reminds you that you already come with a map back to yourself. For me, the chakra system was and continues to be the soulful map guiding me back home to my true self, and I know it holds many blessings and miracles for you too. Chances are, if you are drawn to reading this book, your soul is yearning to seed a new conscious awareness so you can blossom from the inside out and be nurtured by the ever-expanding radiant divine feminine creative light expressing through you—as you. May these words touch a tender sweet spot in your heart and re-attune you to your divine feminine soul song, that quiet felt sense, gentle nudging, and whisper-soft intuitive calling. May you distill your own magical wisdom elixir and drink in spiritual joy until it's pulsating through your veins, vitalizing your life force, and fueling your creativity so you can soar beyond who you THINK you are.

For too long, I was running on empty. I was trying to do it all yet feeling like I was never enough until I started to wake up to the sacred feminine in me. I didn't just wake up one day and have an epiphany. That would have been easier. My morning ritual, many moons ago, started with a "Beep! Beep! Beep!" as I hit the snooze button, bargaining with myself that just ten more minutes was all I needed to face another day. My awakening spanned many a snooze-button moment for years. I would "wake up" only to fall back to sleep (both literally and metaphorically) as I spiraled through my awakening process.

Looking back, I often felt I was straddling two worlds. The pain of being pushed into the splits also pushed me to make some gut-wrenching decisions. While open to my angels and chakras, I still arm-wrestled with my soul, bargained with my guides, squirreled away resentments, and cherry-picked my battles with my then-husband and step-son. I kept myself so busy that I could rationalize avoiding conflict. I told myself the stress would undermine my creative projects that I was pouring my heart and soul into. I avoided creating ripples and instead created a book, a competitive dance routine, a side hustle—a busy creative life. It was balm for my weary, stress-worn soul, and my inner sanctuary where I could express my truth without pushback. It was a beautiful cozy cocoon where I could explore creative self-expression, but over time it became increasingly uncomfortable. Fulfilling my outer role and honoring who I truly was were at odds, the gulf ever-widening.

As family health issues intensified, I slam-danced amongst worry, heartache, confusion, guilt, shame, and concern, slipping into the default role of playing the peacekeeper as I went with the frenzied 'flow'. In a sincere attempt to face up to the messiness in my life and how I was contributing to it, I became aware that the natural caregiver in me had shapeshifted into its toxic twin, the 'caretaker'. My life was littered with coping mechanisms, and these carried me only so far. What began as a rocky boat intensified into a leaky boat, and no matter how much I tried to help "fix" our problems, sinking seemed imminent. Life felt like it was happening to me, rather than for me or through me. How could my angels and chakras help me now?!

Punctuating the moments of panic, an inner nudging had grown stronger in me. Everyone was doing the best they could, given what we knew. I know that now. Yet despite all of us being well-intentioned, the crisis escalated. You can't give what you don't already have. We were all living from empty cups. I had to seriously ask myself if continuing to do life in the mosh pit with them was truly helpful? Looking back now, these challenging times were like fertilizer; rich soul experiences that truly helped me to grow.

Dis-entangling myself from the expectations of others, in an exceptionally difficult situation for all, prompted me to do the most counter-intuitive thing ever—put myself first and travel on my own—not for work but for self-care! I was terrified of the consequences of breaking the "rules" and being seen as selfish. I couldn't recognize then what I know now. I had perceived my SOURCE of security, identity, purpose, safety, and financial stability as being outside of me, which I denied at first. So that's where all my energy went, out horizontally—and that's why I was feeling so depleted.

I packed that piecemeal quilt of frayed passions, incongruent coping patterns, quickly stitched back together loose ends, and I created a woman-cave abroad where I could heal and come to terms with my decision to grieve the loss of the life I was supposed to live. While my inner renegade yearned to yank the loosest thread and unravel it all, the good girl in me resisted such impunity, pleading she didn't want to hurt anyone. Yet, I was hurting. And there was no one looking after me. And when I discovered I had a cluster of cysts in my left breast, that's when it got real fast! I decided once and for all that it's not selfish to practice self-care. I could not give what I didn't have!

Prior to this stressful period, the seed for this inner blossoming had already been planted. Like a haphazardly watered house plant, I hadn't given myself full permission to nurture its growth. Six years before I married, the goddess whispered an opportunity to teach abroad one summer in Cozumel, Mexico. Only once had I been on a plane in my early twenties. Never in a million years did I imagine going to Mexico. I even doubted whether my Canadian constitution could handle the heat!

I laugh as I look back. My unfaltering "Yes!" to the job offer, ignorant of where Cozumel even was, felt curiously different from so many other "yes's" in my life up until then. Those ones were tied to what I perceived others expected from me. I wanted to be seen as good, caring, unselfish, and "perfect" by following a well-trodden path and not daring to go too far off-road. My cautious approach to living and not wanting to make a mistake kept me more focused on pleasing others rather than myself.

That "yes" changed the course of my life! La Isla de Cozumel made quite a first impression on me and is now deeply imprinted on my soul. After checking in at our hotel, our student group clambered onto a tour bus that eventually opened its squeaky doors to the sweltering salt-kissed humidity at the Mayan ruin site, San Gervasio. Our tour guide led us along a winding path beside sun-bleached, rustic stone structures and smudged smoke over us to keep the mosquitos from a feeding frenzy. I felt drawn at once to place my hands on one of the ancient stone monuments that had a pair of red hand marks, feeling an intense desire to connect with its ancient energy. Despite being raised not to touch the artwork in galleries, something came over me. By the tour's end, a female student asked me if I had lost my belt. Surprised by not noticing it had fallen off of my long raspberry broom skirt, I thanked her. As I studied the belt, with its oval leather pieces attached by thick leather threads, my throat caught, and my heart skipped a beat. There had been a scissor-clean cut right down the center of one of the oval pieces?! It defied logic. Therein began a litany of spiritual "a-ha" moments that initiated me into a new way of perceiving reality, and unbeknownst to me at the time, were inviting the goddess into my life.

For close to two decades now, I have followed the magnetic pull back to this sweet spot on Mother Earth even if it raised eyebrows, especially once I started traveling there on my own for "self-care". What force was at play, I wondered? Eventually, I came to realize it was the beautiful Mayan creation moon goddess Ix Chel with her flowing skirt like fertile waters, adorned with fragrant water lilies, jade, and turquoise. Also known as Lady Rainbow, this triple goddess, mother of all the Mayan gods, as well as a healer, weather-keeper, writer, weaver, and beekeeper, was radiating her soul song. Patron Goddess of La Isla Cozumel, historically every year, young women made a pilgrimage by canoe to her temple to ask for her blessings in marriage and childbirth. An awesome rite of passage requiring courage, trust, and faith around the tender age of fourteen. As I mustered courage for my annual pilgrimage by modern ferry from Playa del Carmen to Cozumel, my preparation for choppy waters was ginger Gravol.

Her medicine was exactly what my soul needed to embody deeper self-care. Each time I visited the island, a dormant part of me activated, opened, and started to rebalance, the spirit of place revealing soul truths to me. Despite a part of me still waxing wistful for a traditional life that was crumbling, there was also an emerging expression I couldn't yet articulate wanting to birth through me.

Her island is often referred to by twinkling-eyed locals as a womb, and it is said that she tests tourists who dare to dream of living there long after their cruise ship has left the port. Not eager to be home to dewy-eyed tourists seeking to cast themselves in a selfie driven iMovie version of *Eat, Play, Love*, she requires a stamped passport of your spiritual tenacity, your willingness to recognize the gifts in life's stressors, as well as the humility to be transformed by them. For she too was once initiated through life's ordeals into deep self-care and divine service. When the universe conspired to give me permission to climb to the top of her ancient stone temple, my "yes" overrode my fear of heights, and I surrendered to TRUSTING the moment's gift. After placing a rose quartz heart mid-way up, I sat on top listening for the signs spoken on the wind, dancing warmth around me, in silent meditation:

Beloved Ix Chel, my heartfelt intention is to enter into Sacred Union. I recognize that I have been running away from 'home' and yet I deeply desire to feel at home in my body, soul, and the universe, to feel I AM enough as I AM, and I humbly ask you to guide me to reunion with a sense of my divine worthiness so I can honor my cosmic mission. May this request be fulfilled as gently and wisely as possible for the highest good of all and in alignment with the divine nature and origins of all.

So it is! It is done. It is done! It is done!
Thank you! Thank you! Thank you!
Love you! Love You! Love You!

While her tests and gifts are many more than what I share here—perhaps a few snapshots will prove illuminating. Ix Chel from my heart to yours, I am so very happy and grateful!

Ix Chel invited me to get out of my head and grounded me into my body and root chakra. She tested my beliefs around safety, belonging, and trust. From sweaty salsa dancing to sticky insect stings that oozed puss and give me 'cankles', from scoring my thigh against the side of the dock right before catching a flight to jellyfish stings, and stepping on a sea urchin (and still climbing her temple) she tested my stick-with-it-ness.

Ix Chel guided me to more fun and frolic, leading me off the beaten tourist path to other beautiful feminine souls through ballet, yoga, energy work, snorkeling, massages, ear candling, and cooking with the freshest fruits and veggies. Most of all, she inspired me to slow down, nurture more pleasure, take a more sensuous orientation, and guilt-free naps. Relaxing opened the inner space in my sacral chakra to thaw out the frozen cellular energy from old hurts and habits in the warmth of a renewed passion for living.

Ix Chel activated my soul gifts in my solar plexus chakra, inspiring me to finish writing the draft of my first book *In Rhythm With Your Soul* by suggesting water metaphors, led me to the local Museum to donate Chakradance™ workshops in Spanish, despite my insecurities about my Spanglish, and then enrolled me in Mayan language classes in Spanish to Mayan. She balanced my determination with humility, infusing me with confidence, decisiveness, and a deep desire to serve.

Ix Chel held space for me to stop bottling up old grief, fear, and unexpressed emotions so my heart chakra could heal and open to receiving greater depths of love and friendship. She introduced me to a soulful Scuba guide who helped me overcome my fear of deep water from a near-drowning incident as a child as I learned to trust men to be there for me emotionally. She called me into a Temazcal ceremony with an inspired feminine guide who was so in her heart and in touch with her inner goddess that my fear of being in a hot, enclosed space, transformed into a deeper trust of self and sisterhood.

Ix Chel opened my throat chakra by encouraging me to listen to signs. Her name arose in a polite conversation with a local Mayan artist, experienced with many archaeologists, who led me safely into her sacred jungle sanctuary. As we made our way off-road by pick-up truck, a flock of blue *morphos* (butterflies); a sign she had given me while meditating with her, appeared to dance excitedly, blessing our drive-in. We cut the rest of the way through with a machete to behold the breathtaking cathedral of the earth—Ix Chel's inner jungle womb space.

Ix Chel increased the bandwidth of my third eye chakra to receive spiritual guidance. One evening, I was visited by an etheric dark-haired male shaman with tanned skin, a stocky build, and white loincloth beside my bed, who appeared before a colleague of mine in another room too at the exact same time. This started an unexpected conversation and friendship between a right-brained art teacher and a left-brained math teacher. Later I learned of the hushed island lore about his night visitations. She also led me to a private Mayan Fire Ceremony on the Day of the Elders. The owner of a healing center named after her drove me 70 km from Playa to the Maya Zona. My dream of meeting a real Mayan Priestess expanded into meeting not just one but three of them that day!

Ix Chel invited a deeper crown chakra communion with Spirit through animal totem teachers. From the iguana whose eyes I stared into at length as I stayed in my heart, to the bird in my garden that I nurtured daily trust with until it invited me to gently stroke it, to the spritely orange tabby that befriended me daily and let me remove a splinter from his paw. The Mayan greeting "in lak'ech ala k'in" (I am another you, and you are another me) was the silent telepathic mantra I exchanged with these beings, from my heart to theirs.

Ix Chel aligned my soul star chakra, attuning me to my cosmic mission, including creating a women's Chakradance™ retreat for the women in my Toronto workshops. She inspired a vision of them restoring their sacred feminine creative flow, amplified by the spirit of place, balanced by giving to the local community with humble donations of school supplies and contributing to healing the Earth through a water blessing ceremony with a Mayan Ceremonial Leader. Fireworks resounded in my heart when one of my Chakradance™ clients claimed her "Yes" and came on retreat despite her friend canceling on her. She decided to go alone. Her family needed her. She decided she needed herself too. She trusted that her soul's perfect timing was inviting her on a sacred pilgrimage to heal past hurts, and she let her inner goddess guide her, declaring that self-care isn't selfish; it's loving and responsible.

If you're letting yourself get bumped to the bottom of your to-do list, ask yourself, if someone claimed to love you and would not offer you undivided attention for even 15 minutes a day, how would you feel? If you answered unseen, unheard, unacknowledged, unvalued, then beautiful feminine soul, the one you've been waiting for is you!

If you invite me to guide you, I will show you new ways of being so your "yes" doesn't leave you stressed. By placing your hand in mine, you will take a one-year soulful inner journey, trusting that wherever you are starting from is perfect for what wants to emerge. Let me squeeze your hand through the birth pain, guide your breath through the emotional contractions, and wipe your sweaty brow as you transform struggle into rebirth. May that ineffable truth, beauty, and goodness within you be expressed and received. I will walk beside you to champion your awakening and nurture your inner blossoming each step of the way in the comfort of your own home, on your schedule. Receiving one-on-one monthly medical intuition mentoring will empower you to shift forever how you generate and care for your energy. Opening, activating, and balancing your chakras through guided meditation and ceremony will calm your nervous system, call back your energy from the day, and reconnect you with the unconditional loving guidance of your angels and guides. Committing to your "yes" will empower you to let go of the daily grind one finger at a time as you restore the sacred to your daily life. Expanding your consciousness will remind you that you already have everything you need as an energy being to navigate it all.

All that creative-intuitive divine energy is yours now to collaborate with. That's why your "yes" matters! What so many miss is that on the other side of pain, heartache, and burn-out is true spiritual freedom. You will be amazed at how liberating it feels to clean up the dust bunnies and live from a continuously refilled cup, knowing you have more than enough energy–and are more than enough–to share your gifts with the world.

Experience the Divine Feminine Empowerment difference. Say a soulful "yes" to chakra-care. In my program *Creating Calm in a Crazy World by Balancing Your Chakras,* you come first. Live the inner goddess way so you can shine your love and light even brighter. I invite you to connect with me at: info@pollyannablanco.com and find the creative inspiration and support you need for your sacred feminine awakening journey at www.pollyannablanco.com, Instagram, YouTube.

ABOUT THE AUTHOR

POLLYANNA BLANCO

Pollyanna Blanco knows all too well from her hamster wheel experiences that slowing down, nurturing divine feminine energy, restoring inner harmony, and balancing your chakras offers you the energy and inspiration to live the fullest expression of your vision and mission. She cares deeply about divinely empowering busy creative souls to reconnect with their spiritual resources to transform stress into magic and miracles. She offers chakra wisdom through a medical intuitive lens. She is an Energy Healer, Teacher, Mentor, Author, Chakradance™ Facilitator, City of Toronto Holistic Practitioner, a Samhara™ Reiki Master, Infinity Healing, and Divine Connections Practitioner, along with Sacred Rudraksha, Avesa Balancing, and Ascended Numerology. She is registered with the Canadian Reiki Association, The International Institute of Complementary Therapists, and the Ontario College of Teachers.

She holds a Hon. B.A. with distinction, a B. Ed from U of T. and dances her talk as the North American Imperial Pro-Am Show Dance Spring Tulip Champion at the 2013 Ohio Star Ball.

I invite you to connect with me at: info@pollyannablanco.com and find the creative inspiration and support you need for your sacred feminine awakening journey at

Website: www.pollyannablanco.com
Instagram: pollyannablanco
Youtube: Multidimensional Muse

RABIA SUBHANI

FROM OVERWHELMED PARENT TO OVERJOYED MOTHER: HOW MINDFULNESS AND SELF-COMPASSION TRANSFORMED MY LIFE

The wound is the place where the light enters you. ~ Rumi

*N*o truer words have ever been spoken. A renowned Sufi poet and mystic spoke these words over 800 years ago. And never did I think that they would apply to my life or that Rumi would come to mean so much to me.

By South Asian standards, I was living the life by 2012. I was married to a doctor, one of the two professions accepted by South Asians as a "successful" marriage (the other is an engineer, in case you're wondering); had a beautiful son; and had a lovely house close to both my mother and his parents, who lived in nearby towns. But I had a painful secret. I was deeply unhappy in my marriage. My husband and I had no connection anymore and had drifted apart. But culturally, I was raised to find divorce unacceptable unless I had a *very* good reason (namely, adultery, addiction, etc.,) so I resigned myself to accepting that we'd hit a bad patch in our marriage and would be able to work it out eventually. Ever the eternal optimist.

I felt unfulfilled as a woman, stuck in a marriage with a man I had nothing in common with except our child and similar cultural backgrounds. I longed for fun, playfulness, and affection. In hindsight, I realize I also had postpartum depression, which went undiagnosed. When our son, Aden, was around 3, we realized he had autism. In one of life's greatest ironies, I had specialized in pediatric neuropsychology and, specifically, autism; prior to having a child. However, Aden didn't display the typical red flags I had come to recognize for autism, so he went undiagnosed for a while. I ended up staying at home and working with him till he started school and then went to work. In 2012, I was working part-time, primarily testing children and adults, and Aden was in elementary school.

Unfortunately for me (or rather luckily, as it turns out), my ex very unexpectedly gave me one of those "good" divorce reasons (hint; it wasn't addiction!). I won't go into details but suffice it to say that I ended up going through a rather traumatic divorce, one in which my son was emotionally devastated and would require seven years of therapy from which to begin to heal.

Aden went through so many unexpected changes during the next few years, from parental separation/divorce; moving from his childhood home; starting a new middle school, leaving his friends behind, and then finally, puberty. He was overwhelmed, and this resulted in numerous temper tantrums and behavioral challenges. I had taught mindfulness to Aden when he was around four years old, and he loved the practices. But when all this happened, he was unable to remember or apply anything he had learned. I then tried all the techniques in my professional repertoire, but with little success.

To be perfectly honest, these issues were also made worse because I was not at my emotional best, either, during this time. For the first time in my life, I was questioning my self-worth and wondering what I had done to "fail" at this marriage business. I was also short on patience due to my own stress, so often, Aden and I would end up screaming at each other. I felt shame and guilt that, as a psychologist, I couldn't handle my emotions better and also that I was not showing my child the patience and love he desperately needed. We were both in so much pain, and I knew this couldn't go on.

Overwhelm had taken over our household, and peace seemed far out of reach. My mental resources were so low I didn't know how I could ever be whole again. The constant battles were so emotionally draining, I was depressed and drowning in despair. Life was bleak and unbearable.

One day I happened to stumble across a book that changed my life and was the first of many AHA moments in my life. It was Dying to Be Me by Anita Moorjani. This book opened my eyes to Universal Consciousness—I felt as if I had been living in the Matrix and had finally woken up to the truth of life! It was heady, exciting, and a bit scary. After reading that book and marinating in the lovely juices of this profound knowledge, I made several life-altering decisions.

I decided that if I couldn't change Aden's behaviors, maybe I could change my reaction to his behaviors. This was a pivotal point in my life as I finally embarked on my own spiritual journey—one that led me to embrace mindfulness, self-compassion, joyful living, and ultimately, Sufism.

Knowing I had to heal myself and my own sense of self. I began by devouring books on self-compassion and reciting mantras each morning: may I be kind to myself; may I give myself the grace to get through today; and may I accept myself just as I am. And then moving on to stronger affirmations: I am strong; I am an amazing mom; I am doing the best that I can; and finally, I love you.

During this time, I went traveling—a lot. Traveling was my gift to myself. I had always wanted to travel, but my ex didn't. It was also a respite from parenting and a spiritual journey all in one.

To move, to breathe, to fly, to float,

To gain all while you give,

To roam the roads of lands remote,

To travel is to live.

~Hans Christian Andersen

To continue my personal growth, I went on spiritual retreats and deeply immersed myself in mindfulness practices. And then a shift happened. It wasn't overnight or even over a few months. But there was a shift. In my alignment with peace, love, and compassion, I changed and evolved into a kinder, more patient, and loving person and parent. My angry reactions to my son's behavioral issues become thoughtful responses instead. I approached each challenging situation with much more grace and kindness, both for my son and for myself.

It didn't happen quickly, but it did happen. I remember the first time I noticed how I had changed was when I had an incident while driving in which somebody suddenly cut me off. In the past, I would have cursed and perhaps honked my horn. But the new mindful me considered the driver with compassion and wondered if he had suddenly received bad news or was in a hurry due to a family emergency. It was another one of those AHA moments. I had arrived.

As I mentioned earlier, perhaps the most beautiful discovery was when I began noticing that my parenting interactions had also changed for the better. My kinder, gentler, mindful responses had resulted in a shift in the dynamics. Our interactions were not as stressful anymore because I was allowing some love and compassion into the interaction. I was responding instead of reacting, and it made all the difference. I love this quote by Alexander den Heijer that captures parenting so beautifully:

When a flower doesn't bloom,
you fix the environment in which it grows,
not the flower.

As the days became weeks and then months, my relationship with my son transformed to what I had always hoped it would become; because I had fixed the environment and allowed my son to bloom. The guilt started melting away as I no longer had that icky feeling after one of our screaming matches. Best of all, after doing my own inner work, I was in a place to be a much better parent and give my son the best version of me. I was able to offer more compassionate parenting because I was offering compassion to myself. This is when the magic truly manifested.

While on a silent retreat one day, I had a major epiphany. The reason my son couldn't retain his mindfulness practices when all these changes happened was because I had never done them "with" him. I had taught Aden lots of mindfulness techniques because I thought *he* needed them, *not* me. But how can a child be expected to retain information when he's overwhelmed? And when there is no one to model it for him? This was the crucial piece that had been missing, and I wished someone had taught me how much difference it can make to teach parents about mindfulness to help them practice and model it for their children. Then I thought, "well, why don't I teach that?" It was a radical realization because I had spent so many years learning how to be a neuropsychologist, and now, I had already made the decision to re-train in a completely different field!

But my spiritual journey had left me with several profound insights: one of which was to live life from a place of sublime soul-alignment. Life is too precious to waste on living, being, or doing something which does not speak to your heart. Life is meant to be lived with purpose and passion. My training and profession were not serving this new upgraded version of myself. I wanted to show up authentically in all spheres of my life. I wanted all of me to reflect my newfound zest for living. I had become a joyful, illuminated Being, and everything I did should reflect that.

I invested in myself and began re-training in multiple mindfulness and compassion-based programs so I could teach other parents of neurodiverse children the concepts that had so transformed my own life. I enjoyed every single one, but there was always something missing. I wanted to teach families about mindfulness but also about self-compassion. So many parents of neurodiverse children carry feelings of guilt and shame, always wondering if they are parenting correctly and feeling embarrassed and ashamed when they lose their temper or think they are doing something "wrong." And I wanted these parents to have hope and optimism for the future. It's not enough to teach parents to live in the moment. When you have a neurodiverse child, you need hope for the future, as well. What is life without hope, after all?

This was when I decided that if I couldn't find a program with all the components I wanted, as both a professional and as a parent, I would just have to create one. And Mindful Village® was born. I combined mindfulness with self-compassion, positive psychology, and neuroscience to create an eight-week secular program for parents with neurodiverse children. I wanted to reach as many people as possible, so it became an online program. I am currently working on a non-profit organization that will provide scholarships for those with fewer resources. I also hope to translate this program into multiple languages by the end of the year and have extension modules for various neurodiverse challenges, such as autism, ADHD, and anxiety. A child-focused program will be next on the list.

My spiritual growth and epiphanies didn't just stop at mindful parenting. I have had so many revelations over the past nine years. The most profound one was the realization that I was a Sufi (the mystical aspect of Islam). I had toyed with Sufism in the 90s as my all-time favorite singer was a Sufi qawwali master, Nusrat Fateh Ali Khan. His singing would send me into an ecstatic trance, and I wondered why it had such a profound impact on me. Unfortunately, I was not yet at the stage that I felt comfortable stepping outside of the confines of my more traditional Muslim upbringing.

In 2013, when I started my spiritual journey, I fell in love with Buddhist concepts like loving-kindness and metta, and I absolutely loved meditating. Thich Nhat Hanh was a favorite, and I went to a retreat to Plum Village just to soak up his residual energy! In fact, my favorite mantra that I still say to myself every morning is a quote by him:

Waking up this morning, I smile.
Twenty-four brand new hours are before me.
I vow to live fully in each moment
and to look at all beings with eyes of compassion.

One of my first mindfulness mentors was this absolutely lovely soul, a Buddhist nun named Joanie who had converted from Judaism 30+ years earlier. I was so blessed that she moved to the small town I live in, and I could learn from her! I used to tell my beloved teacher that I thought I was Buddhist. And she would have this beautiful smile on her face and say, "Rabia dear, when you find your spiritual home, your heart will know." She was right.

Fast forward to 2017, and I was watching Super Soul Sundays with Oprah, and she was interviewing a Sufi mystic, Llewellyn Vaughan-Lee. I was intrigued by the short clip and found a longer interview by him on YouTube. As I watched the interview, I was overtaken by a cascade of emotions. I felt stunned and then had an almost out-of-body experience. I started weeping copiously and didn't know where the tears were coming from. My soul was on fire and drowning in love at the same time. I felt tingles all up and down my body. Llewellyn was talking about ME. I felt heard and understood for the first time. Because he was one of the Silent Sufis and practiced meditation; everything was about the heart and Divine Love. God was the Beloved. Everything a Sufi does comes from a place of love. I was a Sufi, and I had finally come home.

This revelation transformed my entire life. Because I now knew what had been missing. I had always known that I was deeply spiritual, but none of the religions as I knew them spoke to my heart. But I was a Sufi and had always been. I had just forgotten for a while. And I rejoiced in that knowledge. I read tons of books on Sufism and spent countless hours exploring the different orders or tariqahs. I was confused because I felt called to many of them. I loved silent meditations from Llewellyn's Naqshbandi order, but I also loved the Chishti order, which used music (like Nusrat Fateh Ali Khan) to reach the Divine. I was also called to the Mevlevi Dervishes, which followed Rumi's teachings and still others which combined several different teachings, like the Inayyatia order.

They felt so far out of reach, and I wanted that personal connection to a teacher. One Sufi teacher, the spiritual leader of a Mevlevi order whose books I really enjoyed, Shaikh Kabir Helminski, seemed more accessible. In 2020, I had the opportunity to go on a writers' retreat to Costa Rica, in which he would be leading the group. I was initially reluctant because I didn't think I'd fit in. Who was I to call myself a writer? But the chance to be with other Sufis for the first time in a lovely setting and with this wonderful teacher was too good to pass up, so I went.

Another pivotal moment in my life arose from this illuminating gathering. First, it was Costa Rica, so I was already half-way to paradise. Second, the people I met there were some of the most beautiful souls it has been my pleasure to meet. They were warm, loving, accepting, and kind. The level of energy you soak up being surrounded by such beings is incomparable. As an aside, this is why I go on so many spiritual retreats! Third, it was an absolute honor to meet Kabir Dede (as he is affectionately called). He was just as warm and lovely to meet in person as you'd expect from reading his books. And he was so humble!. His wife is also a lovely Sufi teacher/author, Camille Helminski. I loved them both.

Finally, I had so many spiritual openings on that week-long trip. It was unbelievable. Kabir Dede said something which completely overrode my impostor syndrome. "We are all poets; poems are the language of our experience." And suddenly, I was a poet. I had never considered myself a writer, but I wrote poetry the whole time I was there. It was like the gates had opened deep inside—I felt like a vessel for the words that flowed out of my consciousness, from my spiritual heart. It was beautiful.

I came back from that trip, not realizing it would be the last trip I took for over a year. COVID-19 had hit while I was basking on the sands of Costa Rica, soaking up all that spiritual energy. But it is possible to be stressed and still find joy in everything. I used the "Year of Covid" to deepen my spiritual practice. **I couldn't go outside, so I went inside.**

What followed were months of spiritual practices, which allowed me to go deep inside and complete a lot of inner healing work. My creative centers were going crazy over the year—I was excitedly involved in learning as much as I could, taking up everything that was available from teachers who were forced to go online. I was thrilled to discover a truly gifted Sufi mystic, Lewis Abdullah Cattell, from the UK, who did daily Facebook meditations. He had a profound impact on my spiritual growth, as well.

I felt a bit guilty in this hedonistic learning frenzy as others were forced to cope with quarantining and were depressed and isolated. As a semi-introvert and a lifelong student, I was in heaven with all the opportunities now available, and I reveled in them! Classes from all over the world were now just a zoom call away. I could sit in retreat at Plum Village again and soak up the live teachings of Rupert Spira or Eckhart Tolle from my study. Kabir Dede's spiritual gatherings, which were usually held in Kentucky, were now online. While everyone else suffered, the world was my oyster. In my wildest dreams, I never imagined I could be so happy when I couldn't travel!

But you know what? During this time of self-reflection, I found that it's not about where you can go or even who you can be with. It's about how comfortable you are in your own skin. How are you showing up for yourself? How much inner work have you done? This quote by Rumi has always spoken to me:

And you.
When will you begin that long journey into yourself?

Dear ones, we must begin that long journey into ourselves if we ever hope to transcend the things holding us back. If we do not do the difficult task of facing our own fears, traumas, and wounds, we will never get to that point where we can be completely soul-aligned with our life's purpose. And yes, we are here for a purpose. Mark Twain once said, "The two most important days in your life are the day you are born, and the day you find out why."

This is my *why*. I am a healer: I fully embrace that and own it. I know with a bone-deep certainty that this is my calling in life. I started healing on a superficial level with my original training as a neuropsychologist, so in some ways, I have always been on this path. But this, the work I do now, is on the soul level. The quantum level. As I have evolved to this Being of joy, I wish nothing more than to bring others to this level, as well.

My fervent desire, my life's journey, is to heal as many people as I can. I want other mothers of neurodiverse children to know that they don't have to be overwhelmed and stressed with parenting issues. Life doesn't have to be so difficult. There is a better way to cope, to live. One that allows you to be at peace, be joyful, and parent compassionately. One that also allows optimism for the future.

And for women in general, I want them to embrace self-compassion and allow grace into their lives. We all struggle with so many issues, but if we could just see that giving ourselves the permission to replenish our soul batteries instead of running on empty makes such a difference. Practice positive affirmations every day if you need, but love yourself unconditionally.

You are meant for so much more than you know. Don't go through life holding yourself back. Spread your wings. Fan that Divine spark inside you. Explore your magic and let it free.

And for everyone, the art of joyful living is such a beautiful practice. Imagine how wonderful life could be if you would allow yourself to see beauty in all the small things and grace in all the big ones. Life doesn't have to be complicated, my friends. It just needs to be lived with love. When you live each day from a place of gratitude and joy, an alchemical transformation takes place in your spiritual heart and in your energy field. Align yourself with abundance, not scarcity. With hope, not despair. With gratitude, not indifference. And above all, with love, not fear.

With life as short as a half-taken breath,
plant nothing but love.
~Rumi

My son didn't suddenly transform into an angelic being. He still has behavioral challenges that come with his diagnosis. But the way those challenges are handled has significantly changed. He is only human (and neurodiverse), so there will always be issues, but there are much better ways to address issues that may arise when you act from a place of love and compassion. My responses to his behaviors have completely transformed our relationship and reduced the overwhelming stress we both had. The energy in our home has become so much more positive and loving as a result. Our lives are vastly different from what they were years ago. We live with hope and ever-present love.

I am not spiritually evolved to where I would like to be one day. But I have evolved, and that is sufficient. It is enough to know that I have come so far from that devastated single mom I was in 2013, blindsided by an unexpected divorce, and left to parent a neurodiverse child on my own. Relinquishing the labels of self-blame and guilt to ones of self-love and acceptance has changed my quantum field to one of positivity. My outlook on life is now one of joy and gratitude instead of helplessness and despair. And my journey has not been an easy one, but it has taught me about empowerment, resilience, and courage. Looking beyond the veil of motherhood, I have overcome and reclaimed my sovereignty as a woman.

Don't you know yet?
It is your light that lights the worlds.
~Rumi

ABOUT THE AUTHOR

RABIA SUBHANI

Rabia is a licensed psychologist and a mindfulness-based life/mindset coach. She originally trained as a neuropsychologist but, after an eventful spiritual journey, became immersed in mindfulness. She was so profoundly impacted by what she learned that she ended up re-training in multiple evidence-based programs so she could teach mindfulness, as well. As the mother of a child with autism, she loves to teach mindful parenting to families with neurodiverse children. She has developed her own program incorporating mindfulness, self-compassion, positive psychology, and neuroscience.

Rabia also enjoys mindfulness-based coaching for women with a special emphasis on parenting, spiritual mentoring, joyful living, and high performance (such as healthcare providers). She coaches with compassion and focuses on long-term personal growth, not quick fixes for short-term issues. Her goal is to help you shift your mindset to align with your life's purpose and live to your maximum potential. You can find more about her coaching and the program she's created, Mindful Village®, at the sites listed below.

Websites: www.DrRabia.com and www.mindfulliving-llc.com
Facebook Groups:
Mindful parenting https://www.facebook.com/groups/mindfullivingllc
Feminine soul-alignment https://www.facebook.com/groups/alchemyheartacademy
Email: rs@drrabia.com

REVA WILD

EROTIC EMBODIED AWAKENING: FROM FEARING REJECTION TO ATTRACTING SOULMATE LOVER(S)

*S*omewhere between the sandbox in kindergarten and our first kiss, we learned that our bodies were not enough for love.

Haunted by the images in magazines, the beautiful girls in our classes, and even our families' comments and half-heard, hushed words around our bodies, we learned that our bodies were not enough for love.
From the strict, absolutely impossible beauty bias, with poised perfection as the ideal, we learned that our bodies were not enough for love.

So many of us as adults still carry this story that our body is standing in the way of us falling in love and experiencing soulmate relationships.

And specifically, that we will never have the soulful, primal, loving, wild, erotic cosmic sex life we've been dreaming of.

This is the one that keeps us up at night. This haunting that feels like a curse.
This bone-deep loneliness from this story of "not enough for love" being repeated over and over.

Those of us connected in the sacred arts of healing, dancing, and playing still find ourselves hiding in plain sight within movement classes, ecstatic dances, and community gatherings. We've gone through deep dive healing ceremonies and intensives and faced so many fears and shadows. We've battled to have glimpses and even deep moments of appreciation and love for the sensations, pleasure, and erotic life current in our bodies. Yet, we are terrified to flirt with the gorgeous long-haired warrior type who's been smiling at us every time we make eye contact with them. Because we are afraid that once again, we will be rejected.

First, the children in school making fun of our thighs, our noses, our bellies.

Then our first crush finding out we liked them and making us feel humiliated with their disgust.

Then, moments of potential relationships leaning in with flirtation...only to ghost and disappear after the first text or the first kiss or the first unsatisfactory fuck.

Rejection.
"I will always be rejected from the love life I want."
This fear of rejection haunts us so strongly that we dim our light and love for life and our deepest dreams seem more and more impossible.

Yet, I'm here to share a different story.
My story.

Titled something along the lines of "the sacred fat goddess who finally fully reclaimed her body and sexiness, fell in love with her queer, kinky, polyamorous soulmate and started saying yes to following all her desires and watched as they all started coming true."

Yes, it's possible, and I'm living it.

Feeling delicious and alive in every curve and roll and edge and line of my body?
Yup.
Flirting with gorgeous humans at ecstatic dances, tantra festivals, and ceremonial gatherings?
Yes, I am.
Saying yes to playful consensual opportunities to dance, touch, and play with other sacred wild souls?
Every moment I can.
Met the love of my life who's primal, kinky, queer, and a sacred plant medicine facilitator who deeply cares about sexual awakening and conscious communication? The one who checks off all the boxes?
Yes, in Guatemala, at a sacred sexuality immersion that catapulted me into the most sacred, soulmate connection of my entire life.

Imagine the most potent and delicious relationship you've ever pictured. A beloved with deep warm eyes and a mischievous smile. Arms that hold you when you fall to your knees with emotion and pin you to walls with a primal, erotic passion that has you spinning into the cosmic womb. A body that dances with yours as lips kiss your sparked aliveness into a gloriously raging inferno. Sacred words, a beautiful mind, cares, and desires that emerge your deepest cares and desires. Playing, laughing, learning through the hard moments of being human together. Dedicated, devoted, and loving beyond what you think you can hold. And the sex...Primal. Powerful. Cosmic. Sacred. Kinky. Succulent. Present. Otherworldly.

Absolutely magickal.

Now, if you're anything like me, the voice you've lived with for as long as you can remember is already telling you that it's impossible. At least, it's impossible for you. Anywhere from a whisper to a yell, this part can sing 8-part harmonies that YOU falling in love, being attractive, and generally living your dream life is absolutely impossible. It does so in hundreds of ways. Yet this is also the deepest dream your precious little girl self has had for as long as you can remember.

Devotedly, the looping thoughts from hell drown this desire beneath their noise.

"Society will never think you're beautiful."
"You're too niche of a wild, spiritual badass to find a match."
"Your body will never be enough for primal, cosmic love."
"Love only exists in movies, and it's never for women who look like me."
"It will simply never happen."

But what if I told you, my Love, that this loop is simply a story you were taught to believe is true. An illusion and your deepest fear masked as the only possible true reality. Yes, there are beauty biases and shame-filled cultural stories around bodies and sexuality. Yet, there is also a grand and rich possibility field around attraction and connection and wild soulmate experiences. And it's possible for you.

I'm going to take you on journey my love, and show you how I and how my clients have also reclaimed their pleasure, power, and sacred erotic desires for partnership. We'll go through my adventure of transforming debilitating body shame and fear of romantic rejection into a thriving relationship with my body and living a wild flirtatious life. I'll share the practices and mindset up-leveling that I share with my clients and utilize daily in alchemizing the shame, fear, and judgement that make flirtation, connection, and deep pleasure next to impossible. And trust me, my love, I'm living it, and it's fucking real.

I was five years old when this loop was first played through me and shook me to my core. I remember sitting in the sandbox with a bright red bucket. My stomach dropping as I looked up to four boys standing over me. I still know the name of the one who said words that would echo through my bones for decades. "You're fat, and you're ugly, and you'll never get married."

I was heartbroken. And this heartbreak would impact me for almost twenty years. Years of the story that my body was not enough for love and relationship piled on from bullying and the media reflecting an impossible image of beauty ingrained the idea that to touch me would be the most disgusting experience someone could have.

One of the most powerful shifts in my body love journey was when I was 14, and I found my first erotic, steamy romance novel. The Immortal Highlander. This was one of the first times I can remember feeling the spark of aliveness in my sex. When my root felt deeply awake and clitoris pulsed with desire even though I blushed every time hearing and reading the words representing my vagina. This was the first time I had felt and heard a romantic story full of passion, sacred ritual, and unwavering devotion, yet it has been singing in my blood ever since.

And it was in talking to a friend about this novel and how aroused and excited I felt by reading these words of sensual heat that I learned I could have that kind of connection with myself. I could offer myself the pleasure that I dreamed of this wild ancient Highlander ravishing me with. I could bring myself to ecstatic states and orgasmic pleasure. Touching my vulva and clitoris for the first time and connecting with this sensitive space of my body was an initiation. I had barely known that this part of my body existed and now I was having visions while experiencing more pleasure than I thought possible. I left my body and fell so deep inside with my profound, anchored presence. I saw the cosmos and images and symbols I would only come to understand in my Reiki Mastery training years later.

For a moment, my body didn't feel like a shameful trap.

For a moment, I tasted what I could only know to be God, Source, the Universe.

For a moment, I was free and alive and powerful.

This experience ignited my determination to understand pleasure, relationships, and sexuality. A few years later, I decided I was going to become a sex therapist, and my purpose and path were anchored. Entering University for my BA in Sexuality, Relationship and Family Studies was only the beginning.

My next initiation into the erotic current of life force was dance. I'd spent years dieting and trying to exercise my way to finally being worthy of relationships. Though dance began for me through childhood classes, when I found a spiritual dance practice in University called GROOVE, I fell deeper into my body again. Just like the first time I touched the sacred portal of my vulva and clitoris, I had orgasmic experiences on the dance floor. Shaking, rolling on the ground, leaping, stomping, and letting the music take me deeper into my body, I found my empowered, flirtatious, and wild aspects of self through dance. I learned what it felt like to slip out of the layers of shame I'd been caged in and feel the fresh breath of freedom in my body that I craved.

This connection with dance reached an entirely different level when I found the ecstatic dance and contact improv dance community. I came home, fully and completely to my body. My thighs, my ass, my belly and my arms, all the parts I had been taught to be disgusted by, we're buzzing with aliveness and pleasure. After dancing in the untamed magic under white tapestries and a cedar chandelier, I felt the primal call of my bones and their beauty to stand in the power and pleasure of this practice for all people. Being fully free to shake, roar and roll around on the ground unleashed my inner wildling and healed the centuries of women being taught to sit still and be quiet that still ran in my blood. I was awake and orgasmic in a way I didn't think was possible and ecstatic dance continues to be a daily nutrient in my embodied pleasure diet.

Yet what really allowed for the power of these embodiment practices to work was alchemizing and transforming the mindset generating the "not enough" thoughts.

A year or so after University and various tantra and conscious communication retreats later, I was snuggling beside one of my favourite humans in the eco community home we'd established. Warm lamps and candles lit the old Victorian style living room decorated with the odd assortment of sacred and eclectic furnishings from our seven-person household. Two large pieces of paper were then taped to the wall with large circle diagrams that would become the basis for building a brand new foundation in my life.

The biggest piece that the maps offered me was recognizing that shame and fear, and judgement sprung from a global, cultural story that had been playing out for over 5000 years. The story? That we are innately not enough. That there is something wrong with me, my body, and my personality, and everyone else has it right. The right/wrong, good/bad trap. Where we've been taught to consistently think we are not enough, always more wrong and bad than good and right.

This ignited me into the deepest alchemy. The mission was lovingly breaking down the right/wrong and good/bad structures in myself that kept me feeling trapped and helpless, and unattractive. I melted this internal guilty "I'm bad" identity and rebuilt a deep understanding of myself as a learner. That it wasn't about right and wrong, it was about alignment, curiosity, and desire. I started truly beginning to believe that I could trust myself and what I deeply wanted.

And the most powerful alchemy that came from anchoring in self-trust and my embodiment of a learner? It was transforming shame around my body, judgement around my attractiveness, and fear of always being rejected into gold. The gold of recognizing these parts as protectors from an old order, an old cultural story I no longer wanted to play in. The parts that desired so much to save me from the pain of rejection yet had me ironically rejecting myself over and over and over again.

The spell was broken when I could see the system and the ways my frayed and exhausted protectors learned to try to keep me safe and loved. In the process of bringing my full emotional range to dance and self-pleasure and alchemize these protectors, I hit the wellspring of love and power beneath the parts that shackled my entire life.

Little by little and seeming also all at once, I broke the chains, and my inner Queen rose from the core of my power.

I chose that going forth in the direction of this life I craved, full of erotic and sacred expression, was the whole point for me. That I wasn't helpless or hopeless, I'd simply learned I was. And I could learn the way to being in the world that felt authentic and alive and connect with the lovers and soulmate(s) I came here to align with.

That was the key in all of this; what really allowed me to sink into the gorgeous sacred erotic life I had always wanted. A final puzzle piece brought every pleasure practice, erotic dance, and primal emotional release session together. The secret thread tied in the collaborative mindset of alchemizing shame, fear, and judgement and healing my trauma in feeling rejected from romantic relationships was recognizing my power to choose.

To choose to feel the gorgeous sensations of my curves and the warmth of my skin.
To choose to dance and writhe and moan and touch myself into ecstatic bliss
To choose to live the story that my desires are possible.
To choose that following my desire is worthwhile even in the face of rejection.

To choose to bring my full aliveness forward and to be brave and flirt when I'm attracted to other souls on this wild adventure.

To choose that I am a learner, I won't get things accurate all the time. I can miss the mark and always aim again. I can keep learning and leaning in and celebrating the aliveness in every moment as I redirect towards what I want.

This became the foundation underneath all of my embodiment facilitation, ritual immersions, and body love and sacred sexuality coaching. This is what clicked years of academic and systemic understanding into place with lived experience and aligned energetic law.

When you are more internally connected with your power and aliveness, you are visibly and viscerally more attractive and more open to receiving connection.

This is what has attracted the most delicious relationships I've ever experienced.
Saying yes to my full, wild, sacred passion made me visible to these gorgeous, wonderful people.

It's funny how when you're not afraid to make eye contact, you can see the ones who also want to look back.

And most magically, the ones who not only look but really see your aliveness, attractiveness, and beauty.

For the love of desire, choose to alchemize your shame, judgement, and fear. Let yourself feel what you feel fully, getting to the roots and what's underneath, and then keep going in the direction that you want.

Dance wildly, eat delicious food, lay in the sun, swim in the ocean, flirt and talk with your favourite people, touch yourself, invite pleasure and orgasmic sensations and show up as your fullest, most authentic, and real expression.

Keep bringing yourself back to your power to choose. To feel what you feel and go in the direction of your deepest desires.

This isn't always easy. I'd be a liar and inauthentic if I didn't share that this isn't always sunshine and orgasms. Choosing to do a pleasure practice when your resistance is coming up and leaning in anyway, even if it's just to fully feel the resistance is a learning curve.

Choosing to stop and really have compassion for yourself when your body shame starts looping and makes it feel scary to flirt, and connection takes standing in our power.

One of my clients shared a story of feeling scared to flirt with a person she was attracted to. We'd started sinking our teeth into the groundwork of this deeper mindset shift and pleasure embodiment, and it was the first time since that she was facing the deep fear of rejection in the face.

The 'what if I haven't learned anything and I actually will be rejected forever' fear.

She avoided the person that night. Yet after leaning into an embodied dance ritual and coaching session together, she recognized that her dream was on the other side of this fear; her dream was in following her desire. Even if it wasn't this time or this person, she realized she had to lean in and start eventually, or it would remain far too uncomfortably comfortable to stay in the same fear pattern of not flirting and rejecting herself first. The next time she saw them, she made a huge shift.

In the moment, she chose to do something different. She invited in the nervous sensation of a protector showing up to save her from rejection, alchemized it into excitement at the possibility of what she wanted being possible, and leapt forwards towards her desire. She invoked the pleasure she felt in her practices. Brought out her full self with all the human pieces and parts and chose to be vulnerable and revealed her attraction. And guess what?

They had a gorgeous flirtatious encounter.

It turned out they weren't compatible in a lot of ways, so it wasn't a soulmate relationship, yet it was a beautiful experience of recognizing her desire and choosing to follow it. Choosing herself and leaning in to see what dreams really are possible. And she's gone on to keep learning how to stay with her turn on and invite deeper this erotic embodied life she's chosen.

An erotic embodied life starts with that choice.

To recognize the story of body shame and fear of 'never being enough for a relationship" as a black hole you're throwing energy into.

To begin alchemizing your protectors from rejection and embodying the pleasure and power practices that create the space for your deep aliveness and erotic life current to flow.

To touch yourself with deep presence and devotional reverence with your body and portal of life and ecstasy. To dance like the wild, free, mother-loving goddess you came here as, in all her sensual, powerful, and sexy forms and faces.

Beloved woman, you can do this.
Even if a thousand voices in you, the protectors, are echoing their shame and judgement and fear stories, you can experience the sacred primal relationship of your dreams.
In your body right now as it is.
With your precious heart and your wild soul.

My deepest desire for you is to remember your power to choose. To remember yourself as a sacred learner in the face of the thundering story that you were born not enough. To anchor yourself deeply in your body as a haven and paradise of sensation and pleasure. That you can love her deeply and marry the cosmos with your breath, sound, and movement. To recognize that it's utterly impossible in a world of billions of people for no one to find you attractive and you to find them attractive as well. Beloved, it is entirely possible to align with soulmate relationships when we spark our deepest aliveness and confidence in ourselves.

So go touch yourself. Go primally, sacredly, and royally fuck yourself into cosmic bliss. Remember that this body allows you to commune with the divine and all of life through your sacred pleasure.

And dance, oh wild woman, go dance and dance and dance. Make your own playlist and rage and sway and jump and shake. Be brave at your gatherings and dance front and center with the bass vibrating through every cell of your being. Feel it all. Invite the pleasure. Drink it in like nectar. Your body is not the problem or the blockage between you and love; it's the gateway and the portal to all your most precious dreams. So go dance yourself to ecstatic pleasure.

And be compassionate with yourself. For over 5000 years of human history, we have been working with this fundamental story that something is innately wrong with us and that everyone else has it all figured out. We are learners. And we can learn to be compassionate with all parts of ourselves and go for our desires because when we do, we attract and align with soulmate relationships.

See where the golden thread of pleasure and following your heart's desires takes you, and seriously send me a letter of the love you find on the way.

I promise the journey of loving your body and awakening your sacred eros is the most pleasure-filled and prosperous quest to align with beloved soulmates. The Universe is simply waiting for your sovereign power to say a full fuck yes to the fullest expression of your erotic embodied life adventure. So what will you choose with this one wild precious life?

ABOUT THE AUTHOR

REVA WILD

Reva Wild is an Erotic Embodiment & Sacred Sexuality Mentor with her BA in Sexuality, Relationship & Family Studies. Teaching in the realms of conscious and tantric relating and body reclamation, she brings a grounded, trauma informed lens to the cosmic erotic playground. A Reiki Master and Transformative Ecstatic Movement facilitator, her work is embodied in somatic and energetic practices that create monumental mindset shifts for her clients to feel vitally attractive, deeply sexy, and grounded in their power to follow their wildest desires. She's currently living in Lake Atitlan, Guatemala, with her beloved organizing sacred sexuality immersions and serving her clients while she makes love with life amidst waterfalls, jungles and volcanoes.

Find me on Instagram @eroticembodied
Message me at thedancingwildfire@gmail.com

SABRINA MABEL NICHOLSON

HONOURING EMOTIONAL ENERGIES WITH SACRED BOUNDARY: THE KEY TO YOUR SOULFUL GARDEN OF EDEN

*Y*our heart of golden light has lived many lifetimes of disappointment and pain.

Your inner child longs to be hugged, seen, and heard by her father.

Your rebellious teenager holds a heavy heart of shame and anger, still wounded by a first romantic partner.

Your mind is filled with constant worries, and your body yearns for a soft, gentle touch.

You are a passionate caregiver, always ready to pour your heart and soul into others.

As the hummingbird's love for nectar nurtures the barren lands stripped by the naive man, your colourful soul waits patiently to chant its sacred soul melody and awaken your human life of soulful prosperity.

This is my personal love story, dedicated to the little girl within you and me who believed unconditional love was not a possibility; to the inner adolescent who did not know how to say no and is still healing anger and shame; and to the human woman who worries and forgets at times her wise, powerful inner authority.

This is for all the women before and after us, who are ready to release the shadows and fears of trauma that haunt us for years and even lifetimes.

This short memoir is my legacy to remind myself and my future child to continuously embrace our divine feminine rights, honour our emotions, and live a life of soulful prosperity through sacred boundaries.

I share these parts of me wholeheartedly to release and heal old universal wounds allowing space for a whole new created journey;

And to all of the past souls who played a part in my life thus far, I thank you and love you, and I am sorry for all times my words caused you pain.

This brings me now, to March of 2020, when Ontario teachers had been striking, and the global pandemic was just weeks away from reaching Toronto. It was a Thursday afternoon, and little did I know my life would transform very soon.

I was pressed against the bookshelf for stability, the loud booming sounds of voices and clashing instruments vibrated through every cell in my body. I could feel the heat of my flushed cheeks and my throat tightening as I held back tears. It was that oh-so-familiar dreadful sensation of danger pulsating through me, the one that makes me want to run, hide, and sob uncontrollably.

"But I can't right now. I need to keep it together," my inner critic demanded. "Remember, one two three, one two three, let's keep breathing deeply to calm our body," said my gentle and soft inner voice.

Suddenly, I tilt my head up, and reality hits me. My thirty grade five and six students were still sitting there calmly, leaning back on their chairs and desks, looking directly at me with genuine concern and worry.

"How do I explain to these young souls that a seemingly normal musical rehearsal is causing me fear and physical upset? How do I explain that I am not crazy without having to divulge that I have complex PTSD?" This was the internal debate occurring within me.

As I stood there trying to decide what was the reasonable yet truthful thing to say, my worst case scenario happened. I began to shake visibly, and large tears formed in the corner of my eyes, slowly rolling down my cheeks.

"This has nothing to do with you," I spat out in panic. "You didn't do anything wrong! My nervous system is overly stressed, and the sounds are causing me to feel physically and emotionally upset. I'm going to go home this afternoon. Please be kind to whoever supervises you. Go to lunch now."

I could barely look at them. I was filled with embarrassment and shame. Although I had openly discussed my past with bouts of depression and anxiety, I had never told my students about my current symptoms of complex PTSD. I would never want to burden and displace my own pain onto them, especially considering the empaths and intuitive souls in my class.

Frances Hodgson Burnett, the author of The Secret Garden—a childhood treasure—once said, "She made herself stronger by fighting with the wind."

The whirlwinds of my life began at the age of five when my beloved parents divorced, a difficult and tender time for all of us. My mother and father were both raised with the fleeting model of lasting love, and I can only imagine how earth-shattering it must have been to have to tell their three young children about their separation. My heart remembers his solemn heavy presence, and her light-hearted innocence fade as they each embarked on their unexpected duty of single parenthood.

And like the summer days of childhood escaping us too quickly, we left our beautiful home in Napierville suddenly, and my journey of silent heartache began without ever really knowing the true meaning of unconditional love. Little did I know, this defining moment would plant a seed of thorns whose roots would take years to untangle.

At the age of sixteen, I had such a strong conviction to fulfill my inner child's desire to mend my parents' relationship by finding that alluring true love. I clung to one that would lead me to a path of darkness.

There were definitely happy moments during those years, but unfortunately, most of it was blurred and forgotten by the memories that hurt me.

Ingrained in the depths of my mind lies his narrative that as a human being, I was inherently evil, selfish, and a liar; printed in my psyche, invisible marks of the sleepless nights, questioning my intentions, morality, and behaviours, starting to be convinced there was an impurity to my mind, heart, and body.

The hardest of all are the vague glimpses of sexual acts I was not ready for but finally agreed to commit because I did not know that I could choose not to.

Many times, I suffered silently, all in the name of the naive notion that I had a societal duty to ensure a future marriage and family.

For most of my late teen years, I experienced constant headaches, stomach pains, and emotional numbness, never understanding that I was experiencing psychological and sexual distress. I was simply convinced there was something inherently wrong with me and that this was how life was meant to be.

When I look back now, I know I was simply a child, in a teenage body, that did not know better. I had yet to understand my own needs, wants, and limits. I believed sharing my problems with others was unacceptable and I kept many secrets. To my childlike knowledge, these hardships were also all part of being in a serious monogamous relationship. My intuition was deeply hidden, my faith was non-existent, and my priority was to study and be a good member of society.

However, this first love left a great imprint on me. At the age of twenty-two, when I found the courage to leave, my trust in the world, myself, and others was deeply shattered, and it was the beginning of a long journey learning to cope with this internalized shame, a lack of a sense of self, and having no boundaries.

What my heart really needed was a nurturing nest of safety, but instead, I spent most of my young woman hood chasing this unfulfilled feeling. This quest to fill this wide gaping hole in my chest was only met with disappointment and more distress: attracting romantic partners who were emotionally distant and preoccupied with their own inner demons; finding myself lost in substance addiction. This was the only coping mechanism that provided a real sense of release from my internally distraught reality.

Sometimes, I ask myself, how did I get through this? And when I look back, I realize school was my saving grace: a place where I could have predictable stability and some sense of safety. My high school teachers were my mentors and guided me towards a future of possibility. I was encouraged to pursue a life as an artist, entrepreneur, philosopher, writer, and of course, a teacher. Their attention and encouragement influenced me greatly, and I know now, the people-pleaser in me strived for those A's to feel worthy, seen, and heard by somebody. Looking back, I understand why I was so inclined to choose a career as a teacher, to become the caregiver I had needed for years.

By my mid-twenties, I had started a secure career as an elementary school teacher and I had become a certified Reiki practitioner about to complete a Master's of Education in Developmental Psychology. However, beneath the societal facade of having it all together, I was constantly suffering silently.

I found myself in 2017 pausing my graduate studies and taking a leave from my teaching contract. I began an unexpected journey across European countries to experience ecstatic techno parties while digging deep into the depths of my soul. This completely irresponsible freedom that lasted nine weeks allowed me to truly discover the divine mother and her garden of Eden.

I met her in the darkness of late Berlin nights when strangers caught a glimpse of her golden angelic light enveloping me, and I reconnected with her power when I pulled Fairy Oracle cards for fellow travelers. She reminded me to use my Reiki healing abilities during quiet moments by the scenic rivers of Belgium and called me all the way to Turkey to resolve confusing heart matters with a past romantic partner. The divine mother's protective light was always there, especially when I fell asleep unintentionally in the middle of a Paris public park or when I spent the night at Barcelona's international airport. When my two feet returned onto Canadian land, I had made a promise to myself to never go back to hurting my mind, heart, and body, and a journey of gentle healing began.

"Two things cannot be in one place. Where you tend a rose, my lad, a thistle cannot grow." - Frances Hodgson Burnett

This is when the divine mother really showed her true colours, leading me to the sacred practice of boundaries.

After my weekly women's early intervention session, I was in my social worker's small corner office and was surprised by her genuine interest in my life story. As I explained to her the frustrating moments from my childhood and adolescence, she looked at me in surprise and said, "You know these incidents were not developmentally appropriate for you to have at your age? All of these events are considered forms of trauma." I looked at her in a daze. Wasn't trauma categorized as a horrific accident like surviving a war or a natural disaster? She went on to inform me about 'lowercase t trauma', and how there was a possibility that my symptoms of depression and anxiety, combined with substance dependence, were all indicators of a mental health condition called complex post traumatic stress syndrome.

When I walked the streets of Toronto that day, I remember feeling a sense of relief. There was nothing inherently wrong with me. I had lived difficult moments that caused all of these emotional disturbances and out-of-character behaviours. Suddenly, I was free. I was not to be blamed nor feel ashamed for all of my difficult feelings, weird body dissociations, and avoidant tendencies. These symptoms were a by-product of circumstances from the past, rather than my biological nature! My whole being shifted from a mindset of hopelessness to a state of inner power.

During those many months at the Mental Health and Addiction Center, that social worker taught me the power of having physical boundaries to create safety, to choose my friends carefully, and to speak assertively, owning my right to ask for what I want and need. I discovered I could feel my emotions in community and that there were mindful ways to protect my own energy by choosing a healthier lifestyle of movement, nurturing foods, and low stress. A light within me began to shine, and the divine universe could see it too.

As Carl Jung once said, "The meeting of two personalities is like the contact of two chemical substances: if there is any reaction, both are transformed." And indeed, this was the case for me. This compounded shift began in the Fall of 2018, at the same time that I returned to full-time teaching, completed my Master of Education in Developmental Psychology, and was certified as a Usui Reiki Master Teacher.

On the twenty-first of September, when mother earth always reveals her sacred harvest, I met Gavan. A tall, handsome Sikh man with many facets to his personality. He was an aspiring model and actor working full-time as an accountant, born in Canada but raised in India. A dancer, the life of the party, and yet serious and moody.

Our first date was not love at first sight, but it was the first time in my life, a man mirrored my journey of self-destruction and loneliness while having a thirst for a soulfully aligned path. He also demonstrated intellect, deep roots in spirituality, emotional kindness, and most importantly, he accepted me unconditionally with all my failures and glory.

There was a uniqueness to this man: he honoured the boundaries I set, listened when I asked him to show empathy in my moments of vulnerability, and quickly learned clear communication. He always surprised me, a real learner of life.

Most importantly, he began to challenge me with his own boundaries. When I acted in controlling ways because of jealousy and insecurity, he would remind me of my higher power. He had this high regard for the potential human being I could be and knew a sacred lioness lived within me. He tried his best to understand my complex PTSD and yet, he still put the responsibility on me to heal my own past as he healed his own masculine and feminine wounds.

Together we gained wisdom and continued to deepen our healing while empowering one another to be the highest version of ourselves. This was the romantic love I had always longed for.

Almost three years later, I am still with Gavan. I have resigned from my permanent teaching position, a decision I made in the first months of the 2020 pandemic.

Through my coaching business, Sacred Soul Melody, I now teach women sacred boundaries to foster a life of soulful prosperity. I guide them through the mindfulness practice of cultivating the soul witness; I model and teach self-kindness; and foster a sacred safe space to honour and release difficult emotions like shame and anger.

During my sacred circles, women have uncovered childhood pain from parental neglect, sexual abuse, and abandonment; and they have shifted through stages of grief, forgiveness, and acceptance to begin the process of becoming their own compassionate caregiver.

Through my energetic chakra classes, clients have spontaneously decided to leave workspaces they hated and took a leap of faith, discovering their own soul calling. All of this has been possible through the power of verbal, emotional, physical, and energetic boundaries.

One of my favourite practices for healing inner child and adolescent wounds is a compassionate visual arts meditation where I guide my clients step-by-step. During this guided process, as they draw their emotions through colours and lines, they shift from a space of anger and sadness to inner stillness. This allows you to safely release emotions while detaching from old stories imprinted in your psyche. This non-verbal technique is incredibly powerful for releasing experiences you were never able to express in words as a child. It also teaches you and me that there is power in vulnerability. As Karla McLaren says, the author of The Language of Emotions[1], "Cry as often as you need to. It's the all-purpose healing balm of the soul."

Indeed, through the embodiment of these sacred emotional practices with roots in spirituality and positive psychology, I have experienced time and time again how releasing emotions freely in a sacred safe space is the key to begin a life of soulful prosperity. By letting go of old energies stored in the body and psyche, you create an opening within yourself to welcome new consciously created realities.

However, it has also become clear to me that without community, it is difficult to sustain the courage it takes to continuously set boundaries and embrace vulnerability, especially in a world where hyper-masculinity dominates. This is why I encourage all of my clients to take part in live interactive workshops, especially at the beginning of their healing journey.

When taking part in a sacred community circle, you experience the power of common humanity that all human beings suffer, and thus, we are not alone in this experience. Among the company of others, you also discover kindred souls like yourself who want to hold and honour a loving space for you. The most exciting of all is the quantum magic that occurs when transforming your being with others. As you learn to forgive, accept and love yourself, this emotional energy is compounded by the simultaneous experience of the community.

The truth of the matter is, when we first learn to tend to our garden, and we don't have the loving accountability of a friend or guide, we lose the habit, and we often find our garden bare. The clients who promise to watch replays of live classes seldomly follow through, nor do they experience the transformations they so wanted and needed. Roses seldomly grow alone because nature intended for us to grow together.

This need for collective unity brings me back to the little girl who was sad because her mom and dad separated, and she thought her family was not going to live a life together.

All she really needed was the permission to cry freely, know that her family was always in her heart, and that heartbreak could be soothed with beautiful lines of colour.

The sixteen year old needed to be held and reassured that there was nothing inherently wrong with her and that sexual consent and boundaries were a sacred birthright to be taught to all.

However, the past is the past, and I choose to live with the fact that those experiences and my conscious journey taught me the integral lesson of tending to my own garden of Eden.

Perhaps, I could have read this wisdom in a book, but we all know that knowledge is not always the answer: life experiences are truly the key to lasting transformation.

And so, I pause, breathe, and take a moment to thank these old parts of me who survived, and that showed me how to begin to thrive by listening to the secrets hidden in the strong winds of life: the wisdom of sacred boundaries and honouring myself wholeheartedly.

A year ago, I thought I would still be teaching and enduring one more year of stress before it would be the right and safe timing to take the next career step. A year ago, my nervous system would make my body shake daily. I would cry constantly and worry about the worst possibilities. I know my partner even contemplated whether he still had the capacity to continue supporting me.

A year ago, I never thought I would be this confident, divinely driven, and capable of constantly creating in the face of not knowing what is next. I never believed I would have registered a soulful business attracting consistent income and that I would be waking up early to sip espresso and journal. I could not imagine finally leading meditations, sacred circles, and celebrating in the evening with a candle-lit bath.

I shared this victory over the past from the bottom of my heart because I want you to know it's possible to have a prosperous soulful life.

I want you to wake up with a rested body, a mind filled with new possibilities, a blissful heart, and a soul that sings its sacred melody as you embark on your destined journey.

I want you to be excited about what you are creating, the conversations you are having, and the concepts you are teaching.

I want you to wake up and know the feeling of transforming the lives around you without having to suffer and that it is your divine birthright to put yourself first and embody your worth.

I am just at the beginning of my soul journey, and sometimes, I momentarily doubt myself and think I am a little late in the game, but in fact, it's never too late to follow your destiny.

The time is now.

Avoid my mistake of waiting for a pandemic to take action. Start today moment by moment. Nurture the soul witness through mindfulness; practice self-kindness daily, and honour your difficult emotions in a sacred safe place where you feel at ease and free.

If you are called to, I also want to personally invite you to share your envisioned life of soulful prosperity with me! You can connect with me via my Instagram @SacredSoulMelody or by email SacredSoulMelody@gmail.com. Whichever medium you prefer, but I would love to receive a letter!

If your soul desires to savour the sacred tools and wisdom that I shared, I invite you to discover my signature offer Breathe With Boundaries: a 90 Day Sacred Series to Shift from a Space of Scarcity to One of Soulful Prosperity through Boundary Mastery. Book a free Clarity Call with me at www.SacredSoulMelody.com

Love and light,
Sabrina Mabel

---

1. https://www.goodreads.com/work/quotes/12694321

ABOUT THE AUTHOR

SABRINA MABEL NICHOLSON

Sabrina Mabel Nicholson, Founder of Sacred Soul Melody and Soulful Students, is a Spiritual Teacher and Queen of Boundary Mastery on a lifelong learning journey. As a Reflector by Human Design, she uses her unique abilities to sample auras and capture a woman's untapped power to help her end the cycle of compassion burnout and shift towards an aligned life of soulful prosperity. Sabrina also supports caregivers and their children through a whole child approach honouring the mind, body, heart, and soul. As a certified Usui Reiki Teacher with a Master of Education in Developmental Psychology, she utilises a variety of healing modalities such as Mindful Compassion, Reiki, Intuitive Arts, and Emotional Boundary Mastery. Sabrina's lifelong commitment is to bridge the gap between spirituality and positive psychology to bring a holistic healing approach to broader communities while destigmatizing addiction and mental health issues through the power of story and vulnerability.

Website: www.SacredSoulMelody.com
Instagram: @SacredSoulMelody
Email: SacredSoulMelody@gmail.com

SACHA BRYCE

CORE SOUL WORK: ONE WOMAN'S JOURNEY
FROM FEAR TO FREEDOM

*I*n experiencing life as a child, I remember feeling wise beyond my years but trapped in the vessel of a small person's body who was always being told what was considered "okay" and what wasn't. I was raised within a family that belonged to the Jehovah's Witness religious organization that had a very structured set of rules for what was considered right and wrong, good and bad, which from a very young age I longed to be free from. And as the innocent child's wisdom carries the boundless desire to share unapologetically, to dance and sing without constriction... the unhealed wounds of traumatized adults often unintentionally contaminate the magical potency of this freedom. The patterns of pain become imprinted in the child's subconscious belief system, creating fear-based perceived limitations and blockages to freedom of expression, love, and connection for the course of most adult's lives. I now understand I am here to continue to unravel these limitations for not only myself but for others - so that we may all return to the sacred place of limitless freedom, limitless possibility, and limitless potential - in which no one here is excluded from.

"Out beyond ideas of wrongdoing and rightdoing, there is a field.

I'll meet you there."

-Rumi

My story is one of a highly sensitive and intuitive child transitioning into womanhood and living a life in service to others. They say once you see something, you cannot "unsee it," and I now know this to be true. I woke up at the age of 21 years old in the midst of a 5-year committed monogamous relationship with a young man whom I had met in high school. Together we were heading down the tight tracks of a path that had been laid before us by our parents, and our parent's parents, and our parents' parents' parents. This narrative of what it means to live a socially acceptable, normative, and successful life that I know you who are reading this, are very familiar with. First you must find a compatible and secure partner, commit to a life together, marriage, kids, and the whole white picket fence. And by taking these steps, you are somehow guaranteed to be labelled and perceived as a "success" here. The beating heart of my inner child was quietly but forcefully screaming to me, "There is more for you here!"... "You didn't come here for normalcy!"... "You came here for more!"

And with the conditioning that was at that time ruling my mind and my life, "more" felt selfish, "more" felt greedy, and "more" felt like a whole lot of pain. However, I could not silence the sacred whispers of my heart, or I knew my blood would boil from beneath my skin until one day burning the whole pretty picture into ashes, for not only myself but everyone else that was involved. I knew there was no easy alternative path, but I also knew that I needed to get out of the one I was on.

This was a moment of time in my life where I recognized the power of the choice that I had to make. It's as if the possibility of free will had been turned on, and there was now a switch presented to me that I could flip if I chose to. The options were either to listen to myself or listen to others to inform the rest of my own life. To stay as a damsel in the arms of security or to leap into the unknown with deep trust in the safety that could be sourced from within. I still didn't know where I was really from or where I truly belonged, but I knew it wasn't that which was being presented to me as my only option.

"Life is either a daring adventure or nothing at all."

-Helen Keller

Helen Keller's words began to inform every choice that was required of me to make. It all seemed to boil down to either a great leap of adventure, faith, and mystery and or simply the safe choice: the choice that felt like nothing at all. Without realizing what I had really signed up for, I headed out on a soul's pilgrimage across the world to discover the depths of places inside myself that only I could reclaim. What if the pages were already all written for your life and all that was required was the willingness to put the pen to the paper? Every single step along the journey, it felt like I was guided by a force much more powerful than my own small human body or the limited capacity of this one mind. As I stepped further and further away from the security of what was "known" to me, it became so obvious that I was a part of something unfathomably limitless... unfathomably unknown.

And only until I started choosing the less comfortable options was I able to see how protected and guided I truly was along the path. In the current modern times of restricted and limited travel in the global covid pandemic, I realize the immense privilege it was to live in eco-communities in California and Costa Rica, in Ashrams in India and Nepal, and to sit with Buddhist monks in silent meditation retreats across Thailand and Cambodia... but the truth is you do not have to go far. The truth is you do not have to go anywhere at all. Finding yourself is an inside job, and nothing outside of you will ever have the capacity that you hold to unlock the keys to the inner kingdom.

"The same force that guides the stars guides you too."

My first stop was Australia. I was studying Psychology at the University of Sydney while simultaneously being blessed to land in the arms of a shared home with conscious individuals that shaped the remaining course of my life forever. These four women became pillars in the foundation of the discovery of my inner home. They taught me about reincarnation and about meditation... things I had never even heard of before. I knew these were people I needed to meet and that we would remain friends for this lifetime. I will never forget one of my housemates, Bess, who handed me the book "Many Lives, Many Masters," which completely blew my heart open into understanding the vast infinity of our souls' evolution from body to body... how our life does not end when this body dies. When I had returned home to Toronto after an adventure of travelling with her and her family to Greece, I got the news that Bess and her mother had suddenly died in a tragic plane crash. This shifted my paradigm of what life meant forever as I tangibly knew she wasn't actually gone. She had taught me that. Suddenly it all became so real, as Bess was still with me but now taking shape in a new form.

As perceivably limited beings in these temporary bodies, we have a very difficult time with death and change. The feeling of the pain that inevitably comes with this human experience. We become attached to things as they are, and we don't like to feel the discomfort that comes when they change. I learned through this experience that as we get quiet and sit with nature (that we are not separate from)... we see that death is an inevitable transformation for everything that lives.

And yes, there was pain and discomfort: Pain of the separation from my partner, pain of the loss of my dear friend. As psychologist Susan David puts it: "Discomfort is the price of admission for a meaningful life."

Today I can see the full circle picture of where the path of pain can transform into the path of purpose. I believe we are all here to be of service. We are all here to share the lessons of our own unique experiences to heal one another. Your pain is not for nothing, and your pain is not actually only yours; it carves out pathways and openings for new possibilities of growth for everyone here if you allow it. Expansion is never possible without the contraction, and this is what we are all born from. My journey was one of deep healing and growth, which naturally unfolded into wanting to spill over these teachings and possibilities of healing with everyone that I could reach.

"We can only awaken in others what is alive in us."

At 17 years old, I already knew something wasn't right with the traditional path of being funneled straight from high school to University. As all my friends went off to their studies, I took a year off as an act of refusal to follow "the sheep" of everyone else's path, and I ended up becoming a full-time nanny. I quickly realized the limitations that felt 'oh so real' as I stumbled around in an attempt to be a functional independent adult in this world. I recognized that what I knew was very limited, but I had a strong pull and desire to do meaningful work in the world. I had no idea how or where to start, though I knew I needed to study myself, and I needed to also study other people. This was about the extent of things that I knew at age 17.

The seemingly best option at that time was to walk down the path of education and begin with a degree in Psychology at the University of Toronto. I now strongly know that I learned more from my personal experiences than I did in four years of intensive studies at University. However, this catalyzed opportunities for me that otherwise did not seem available. For many years, I debated going back to complete my master's degree and become a registered clinical Psychologist. As one of my friends said: "Never back, always forward." Something in my heart did not feel aligned with these rigid educational structures. I had to keep asking if the desire to study was coming from fear and scarcity, and in order to be recognized as "legitimate" through acquiring another qualification, or was it coming from a place of excitement, a place of love? These are the only two choices that we are ever truly faced with in life: fear or love.

There is a vital piece missing for me in these types of educational settings, which I now understand to be the wisdom of intuition and embodiment, the wisdom of the divine feminine. I decided to commit to learning from true masters and teachers that I felt awe-inspired by in my own body and soul. I became a holistic yoga therapist and continued to dive deeper into somatic therapy and healing work from there. I began to understand the meaning of following your passions until they become your purpose. And there was no longer the option of working in a "traditional job" or living in relationships that were not in alignment with my soul's highest service. This one life was not long enough to settle for these fear-based options. Something greater than myself, we can call it God, or we can call it love, was now the lighthouse for my life's direction.

I cannot express how joyous and fulfilling it truly is to do healing work with others that feels aligned with your own soul. I have a deep mission to inspire others to find their soul's purpose and to generate abundance in doing so. I believe women will change the world by becoming independently wealthy, doing impactful and meaningful work that they love.

I am honoured to be a facilitator of healing as an Emotional Freedom Technique (EFT) Tapping Practitioner and Trainer. It is now commonplace knowledge that we are made up of energy, and indeed it is proven that we are all connected through the Quantum field that connects all of life. In EFT, we use the maps of ancient wisdom found in Traditional Chinese Medicine and through meridian point body tapping, we process unintegrated energy held in the body from Trauma. This is an accessible and potent way to allow the energy to move through our body and for our nervous systems to regulate and return to a place of safety and home, beyond our trauma and our fear. My work is designed to empower others to hold themselves with love and compassion through all the divine fluctuations that inevitably come with being a human. I love guiding women in ways to find ease in riding the waves of this emotional human life.

I teach women to step into higher levels of leadership and hold space for other people to heal through personal transformation. I train women to walk themselves through their personal development work as the path to become certified practitioners of tapping modalities and facilitators to be of service to others' healing journeys.

WHY EFT MERIDIAN POINT BODY TAPPING?

My mother first introduced me to meridian point body tapping at age eight. She was diving into her own holistic wellness education and was in school to become a Certified Holistic Nutritionist. There was always an interesting juxtaposition in my family where my parents were almost like mad rebellious hippies who also had a strong dedication towards Religion. To give you a few examples, they chose not to vaccinate us as children, and my mother birthed my sister and me at home with no medical interventions. As a young woman, my mother watched her own father become crippled by colon cancer. She painfully witnessed him fade away with the assistance of medical treatments on her family's couch with her three younger triplet siblings running around the house in complete chaos. She drew the conclusion that there had to be a better way to prevent this mess and to treat it - when and if - it does unfortunately arise. She became dedicated to health and healing at a very young age and became my first teacher.

She ended up channelling her own modality of healing known as The Clearing Work ™. This is a unique method of tapping that involves subconscious clearing of limiting beliefs held in the body from early childhood. As Einstein says, "you can't solve problems with the same thinking that created them." This work provides people with a deeper way of healing beyond the limitations of the stories held in our minds. After my five year journey across the world to find my own methods of healing, I remember sitting on the couch back home in Toronto with my mother and her asking me, "So... are you ready to learn my work yet?"

"When you realize how perfect everything is, you will tilt your head back and laugh at the sky."

-Buddha

I did indeed laugh, as I would never have imagined travelling all across the world to come back to what was always right in front of me, available to me, for the lowest cost of admission: free! But the divine time had come, and I knew that I needed to go on my own journey first before being able to learn from my mother.

The most hilarious part about walking on this path is that it is infinite. To think you have arrived somewhere is a fallacy of the mind. I am still arriving every day in this life and am still faced with similar choices. There are a few key differences to my life now, as I feel I have stepped into the space of an empowered woman- a woman on a mission to awaken others to their power. I recognize that nothing outside of myself will ever have the answers, and when you source the wisdom from within, this life is nothing short of magic.

You must know that anything you can imagine creating in your mind is possible here in this life. If you ever wonder why you came here, don't stop there... know there IS more... there is always more. Keep following the things that scare you, and your growth and evolution of consciousness are inevitable.

I met my current partner at an EFT Tapping Practitioner Training. After seven years of being single after leaving my high school five-year relationship, I finally allowed someone new in. People who know me well think it's quite comical that it took the will of God for me to be in the role of client to a practitioner to let a man in again, to let this man in. After years of being together now, it is clear that our souls have met to help each other grow and expand. We openly allow in new possibilities every single day by being dedicated to awakening our hearts to love and practicing noticing the thoughts and patterns that arise from fear. There were moments at the beginning of our relationship where my inner child was begging for more of my own attention, and I would project that onto begging him for attention. This allowed me to deepen my relationship with my own little girl, knowing only I can soothe her at the deepest levels that she needs... no one else. I learned to see other people and my clients through this lens of understanding that there is an inner child inside of them that so desperately wants to be acknowledged.

> *"Tell me, what else should I have done? Doesn't everything die at last and too soon? Tell me, what is it you plan to do with your one wild and precious life?"*
>
> *- Mary Oliver*

I have big dreams and visions of what this life could look like when more of humanity awakens beyond the toxic masculine structures that are currently running "the show" of humanity. I am committing to being a part of the change. I am committed to leaning in and saying yes to life. I am committed to loving myself and others as much as possible for this short human experience. And above and beyond all, I am committed to the path of awakening beyond the limitations of this ego and this self-proclaimed suffering that simply does not have to be holding the torch of power here.

You hold the keys to the inner kingdom. What will you choose?

Go beyond,
Go beyond,
Go beyond.
All of us, let's go beyond.

All the way to the other shore.
-Heart Sutra

No one goes without everyone going.
We rise together in love.
Sacha

ABOUT THE AUTHOR

SACHA BRYCE

Sacha Bryce RYT BSc is the founder of Core Soul Work and the creator of the Core Clarity Certification Training program. She guides women to become practitioners of meridian point body tapping modalities: EFT Emotional Freedom Techniques and The Clearing Work.™ Sacha studied Psychology at the University of Toronto in her home city and abroad at the University of Sydney, Australia, and Edinburgh, Scotland. She completed Holistic Yoga Therapy training in India, Thailand, and Denmark. She is a highly sensitive soul who loves inspiring women to awaken to their inner authority, power, and freedom. She guides women to find their own voice and full expression in the world beyond their blockages from subconscious childhood programs rooted in fear.

Instagram: @sachabryce.eft
Email: Sacha.bryce@gmail.com
Core Clarity Circle: EFT Tapping Facebook Group: https://www.facebook.com/groups/802281226962195

TANYA LEBLANC

THE EMBODIED AND AWAKENED FEMININE:
A SUBLIME LOVE STORY

*E*very woman is born with an incredible source of power. This power lives within her own body. Our deepest healing lives within this realm. The body, the physical and the manifest world are in the realm of the Deep and Sacred Feminine. When a woman has the courage to look within herself, she will meet the Goddess. When a woman has the courage to face her fears, she will meet the Goddess, and when a woman has the courage to heal her shadow, she will meet the Goddess.

Many years ago, I had a profound awakening that changed the course of my life forever. I was stuck in an emotionally draining relationship, and I didn't have the strength or courage to leave. I was so young and insecure, and I didn't feel worthy. I had also just lost our baby, and I felt so alone. The loss and pain were so unbearable. I cried myself to sleep every single night. I cried, and I prayed for courage. I cried and prayed for a way out of this pain, and I cried for that little girl inside of me, the one that didn't feel loved and who felt as if her whole world was crashing around her. I needed to leave this relationship, but I didn't have the strength or power to do so, that was until I met Shakti and the power of the Sacred Feminine.

I remember clearly, it was a cool, rainy morning as thunder rolled deep in the dark sky. The falling rain reflected my inner world as I waited for the next moan of thunder. I stayed in bed and felt a small comfort of peace as the sky rumbled, stirring something inside of me. When I opened my eyes, I heard a familiar voice in the living room. Curious, I rolled out of bed to see who was there and, to my delight, saw my favourite uncle as I peeked outside of my bedroom door. I had not seen him since I was a little girl, but this time I felt a kinship that I never felt before. He was a different man than when I remembered him, as he spoke of Shirley MacClaine, meditation, and the spirit world. It was the year 1990, and this topic was not an everyday conversation at that time, yet I resonated with everything he said and wanted to know more. He handed me his set of tarot cards, and I shuffled the deck. I chose the Queen of Cups reversed and the Seven of Wands.

The Queen of Cups reversed reveals a changeable and over-emotional woman. Sometimes this position signifies a woman who has sustained painful and emotional wounds. She may be locked into an unhappy and unfulfilling relationship, and her talents lie dormant. Although she instinctively knows they are there and should be used, she does not know how to bring them about.

I sat for a moment and contemplated my reading as the message from the cards was so clear, but I didn't know what to do as I felt stuck and torn. My uncle encouraged me to learn to meditate to find my answers. Something stirred within my soul. Could this be the answer I've been praying for? Everything made sense, and for the first time in years, I saw a glimpse of hope on the horizon. I was excited to find out more.

For the first few nights, I breathed in white light and waited for something to happen, but instead of receiving any answers, I fell asleep both times. On the third night of my practice, I thought to give it one last try. This time I was able to let go of my scattered thoughts and clear my mind and felt something shift from the two nights before. I followed and watched my breath, and I imagined my body filling up with white light. I completely surrendered and went into a space of oneness. Then suddenly, I felt my body rock from side to side, and a small vibration moved up and down my spine like a rippling stream of water. The ripple moved up and down, fluttering back and forth, becoming stronger with each undulation. Then all of a sudden, the ripple turned into a massive wave of the most profound feeling of love I have ever felt in my life! This sublime love was total and complete, compassionate, and so pure. Tears of joy flowed from my eyes as ecstasy ignited and filled every cell in my body. I was overflowing with divine love. I was in heaven and embodied pure bliss. I was never the same again.

I soon discovered that this irresistible presence was the sublime love of Kundalini Shakti in her form as Lalita Tripura Sundari. Lalita is the Goddess of Sublime Pleasure and Divine Bliss, and she is the Fulfiller of Desire. The Lalita Shakti lives within the crown chakra and is known as the Supreme Consciousness. She awakens when Kundalini rises up the spine to meet her counterpart Shiva (Sacred Masculine). This was my first encounter with the power of the Sacred Feminine, and this awakening changed my life forever.

The power of the Goddess made herself known to me as she heard my cries for transformation and healing and my longing for love. I was transformed overnight and immediately went on a journey of deep spiritual exploration. My life completely shifted, and I finally had the strength and power to leave my relationship. Instead, I developed a new relationship with myself and my soul, one of self-love and so much compassion. I began to learn and uncover so much about myself, diving deep into the layers of my psyche and the world of spirit. My intuition heightened, I had psychic visions, I saw chakras and auras with my own eyes, and I started to communicate with a spirit guide. I wanted to know everything I could about this world and I was on a mission to find my purpose. Meditation became my sacred practice, and I communicated with the Goddess every day.

One day while in meditation, I had a vision of the most beautiful woman. She was magnificent beyond measure with long flowing dark hair, adorned in red and gold, with many arms and riding a lion. I didn't know who she was at the time, but her image stayed within my psyche, and I embodied her love for days.

In 1997 I went on my first trip to India. The Goddess was calling, and I could feel her whispering to the heart of my soul. Since I was a young girl, I had a fascination with India, and when I landed there, it was like walking into another place in time. It felt as if I had arrived home. The power of Shakti permeated the air, but I didn't know at that time that my relationship with the Goddess was about to deepen.

On that journey, Kali the Dark Mother began to appear to me. I saw her idols and images everywhere and felt a strange connection to this fierce looking being. I admired her power and strength, and her see right through you kind of attitude, and although she was frightening to look at, I sensed her power and motherly love. I then discovered that Kali formed from the forehead of the Warrior Goddess Durga, the beautiful woman in my vision. Mother Durga is the Goddess of Spiritual Strength and Remover of Difficulties and can be invoked for strength and courage. She is the Dispeller of Fear and known as the Unconquerable One. Over the years, Durga has become my Ishta Devi, my personal Shakti, and cherished Goddess.

One night while living in Goa, I had a powerful experience with her. In our bedroom, there was a Jesus Shrine up on the wall, and I was drawn to meditate with it. I gazed directly into the shrine, and soon my vision started to blur, and my body began to tingle all over. The shrine began to take shape and suddenly transformed into a life-sized Buddha, then morphed moments later into Mother Durga. I was completely swept away by her presence. She was breathtakingly beautiful as she looked into my eyes, sending her strength and love. My heart burst open as I received her transmission, but I became so overwhelmed by her presence, I had to break away from the vision. I then let out the biggest cry. I could feel her embrace as I surrendered my tears. Her love was beyond describable. The power of her Shakti is an incredible force, and I know that I had lifetimes of devotion to her.

Shakti is the Sanskrit word for Feminine Power, Divine Feminine, and Feminine Consciousness. She is the Primordial Cosmic Energy and the personification of the Sacred Feminine. Shakti is everywhere in India and is a central part of life there. She is ancient and primal, and some believe she is older than God. In the Tantric tradition, when Shakti unites with Shiva (Sacred Masculine), it is she who is the Supreme Consciousness and Creator. The highest aim and desire in Tantra is to reach God, but the way to reach him is to access the body and wisdom of the Goddess.

Shakti is also the consciousness of our physical world, and even though we live in this world, we are so afraid to descend, to plunge into the emotional waters of our bodies, and into the Deep Feminine. We have become so attached to the mind that we have forgotten how to listen to the body. We also have not been taught to love our bodies, to listen to its wisdom, and to honour the Sacred Feminine, yet her power, her magic runs deep within the DNA of our cells. The Sacred Feminine is part of our inherent nature.

The Deep Feminine also lives within the realm of our shadow, and I have met her many times. The shadow is where our deepest healing lives and is a place that many of us do not want to go or see. The Dark Mother, also known as the Goddess Kali, lives within the shadow, and her purpose is to help us clear our karmic imprints and patterns. Her fierce love takes us to our most painful wounds so that we can transcend and heal, but we can embody her power too when we need to let out a good roar or make some serious boundaries.

In my most difficult and karmic relationship, my inner Kali was in a constant state of rage. I spent two years with a controlling, narcissistic, and self-proclaimed medicine man, and when he showed his true colours it was too late. He had moved into my home, took over my life, and tried to control me, but Kali would not stand for it, and we fought all the time, leaving me completely drained and exhausted.

Once again, I needed to find a way out of a relationship, and once again, it was Durga who saved me. One night she appeared to me clearly in a dream; her beautiful face and eyes looked directly into mine. I knew from the depths of my soul she wanted me to leave, so I ran away from this man, left my beautiful home, and went back to India for the third time. Durga breathed life into me again and gave me her strength, confidence, and power. On that trip, I went back to study at my school, *The Shakti School of Dance*, but I also created my company *Love Not Fear*, and it was Mother Durga who helped make it happen. She is also known as the embodiment of profound love and the remover and dispeller of fear, so I named my company after her. My path of service finally began to take direction and shape after all of these years. *Thank you, Mother Durga. I deeply love and appreciate you.*

A woman's body is a vehicle of extraordinary power, especially when she learns how to receive from the Sacred Feminine. Women were once honoured and revered for their sexuality and natural ability to create, but their power and wisdom was also feared, and this was because the Patriarchy wanted to relinquish control. Instead of honouring her, loving her, and letting her dance wildly, they dismantled and demonized her. They couldn't control a woman who was wild in her power. What a different world it would be if we honoured women's bodies as the embodiment of the Sacred Feminine.

The most powerful energy that we can access in the body is the serpentine energy of the Kundalini Shakti, who lives within the Muladhara Chakra at the base of our spine. Kundalini is a symbol of creative life-force, energy, and sexual power. The serpent is also associated with the oldest known rituals known to mankind, all associated with the Goddess. It represents fertility, creative life-force, rebirth, transformation, healing, wisdom, and power. I am convinced that the serpent in the Garden of Eden is the Kundalini Shakti. Our bodies are designed not only for procreation; they are made for pleasure and to find our way home back to God. The Book of Genesis was truly depicting the Fall of the Goddess and written by men who were afraid of her power. When I had my Kundalini awakening, she empowered me and took me out of the depths of my despair. I was no longer an insecure and unworthy girl. Instead, I became a powerful and awakened young woman. This is why the Goddess is rising. She is coming back to heal our world.

The power of the Sacred Feminine is life itself, and she is the life force within and all around us. When we invoke her, she gives us strength, love, healing, and wisdom. We can access her wisdom through our bodies and through our senses. We can feel her, taste her, touch her, see her, smell her and hear her. She is a living, breathing, and tangible thing, and we can access her at any time, especially when we dance. Dance can be a ritual of cathartic release and is a sacred act of healing. Dance is also one of the most profound embodiment practices and a direct link to Source. When we dance, we embody the power of the Goddess. All we have to do is go within and invoke her. This is the path of the Sacred Feminine. It is the way home to the Divine.

A common theme in the world of the feminine is death, renewal, and rebirth. The Goddess is rebirthing right now. She is coming out of her dark moon phase just as I am entering mine. As I enter into my Wise Woman years, this transitional phase can be one of the most difficult journeys in a woman's life, as we must surrender our youth, contemplate on mid-life, and our bodies go through such a big change. The phase between Mother and Crone is rarely spoken about in today's society, yet this stage was once honoured and revered as a time of transition and marked the birth of a new cycle. It was a stage of initiation for a woman to become fully embodied in her wisdom, and she had the support of her community.

Each phase of a woman's life is a rite of passage, but today we live in a culture obsessed with youth, where we praise the Maiden and Mother while the Crone has been shunned and feared. Instead of embracing maturing women, we are still disregarding them. Today there are many circles and ceremonies for women, filled with beautiful, embodied goddesses in their Maiden and Mother phase, but where are all the Crones? The Wise Women are missing in these circles, especially for women going through her transitional stage. A common need for a woman in this stage is guidance for her changing body.

The Grandmothers, Abuelitas, and Wise Women are in abundance at the Danza de la Luna circle, a traditional Nahuatl (Aztec) ceremony in Mexico that I have been part of for the last six years. The Moondance is the Red Warrior Path of the Deep Feminine and is the most difficult ceremony I have ever experienced. For four nights, we fast, we pray, we sweat, we cleanse, we cry, we sing all night, and we dance. We have the support and counsel of the grandmothers, and of all the women initiated before us. The moon is also known as the Grandmother and is revered in all Indigenous communities. I have never attended any other circle or ceremony with so much Wise Woman wisdom. These women are a powerful force of nature.

On my first trip to India, I spent a day walking the coast of the empty shoreline in Goa with a passionate and striking woman. She was in her Wise Woman years and had been going to Goa every year since the late 60's. She was one of the *originals* they called themselves, the first hippies and westerners making Goa their home. Brita and I walked for hours, and we didn't see another soul all day. We collected shells and ate fresh coconut that she cut with her own knife. She was like a wise warrior who truly had no fear. The lines on her face showed her wisdom, but she was beautiful and young at heart. We talked about life and love, and I learned much from her that day. I remember she said something profound, "When a woman first bleeds, she meets her power, and then she goes through life and practices her power. She has lovers and heartaches, but she grows and learns. But when she stops bleeding and becomes the Crone, this is when she becomes her power. All of her wisdom is now embodied."

At this point in life, a woman's task and purpose is to share her soul's wisdom, but as much as I embrace this stage, it is still a challenging journey. I am in the process of a deep and intense surrendering as I am experiencing death and rebirth at the same time. I am on another journey into the Deep Feminine. I must go back into my shadow for some healing. I am finally in a relationship with a wonderful man, but my soul is deeply craving some space and solo time, and as I write this chapter Mother Kali, the Greatest Crone, just showed me how much I need this space for my transformation. The Goddess is calling me home to help me through this transitional time. Sometimes we need to descend in order to ascend. This is my sublime love story~ a never-ending journey to the divine.

Women of the world, it is time.
It is time for all of us to rise.
Your heart is a prayer.
Your body is a temple.
Are you ready to stand up and RISE?

Women of the world, it is time.
It is time for all of us to shine.
Your body is a gateway.
Your power is your womb.
Sisters it is time to RISE!

It is time to rage and howl at the moon.
We are wild.
We are worthy.

We are wise.
Are you ready to stand tall, with your feet on the ground?
Are you ready to stand up and RISE?

Reclaim your truth.
Reclaim your purpose.
Reclaim the stories of the past.
You are worthy.
You are beautiful.
You are so Divine.
Sisters, it is time to RISE!

Women of the world, it is time.
It is time to hold each other up high!
We are the medicine.
We are the keepers.
We are the caretakers of this land.
It is time sisters, together let's RISE!

When we rise we are powerful.
We are a force of nature.
We are collectively empowered and strong.
Are you ready to stand?
Are you ready to rise?
Woman of the world it is time.

You are powerful.
You are lovable.
You are a magnetic force.
You are an integral part of existence.
It is time to sing.
It is time to dance.
Dear sister, take my hand and let's RISE!

Women of the world, it is time to embody the power of the Sacred Feminine. Her power lives within your own heart and your own beautiful body, and you can access her right now. Slow down, breathe and go deep within. Invoke her and chant her name. Invite her into your heart and listen to the wisdom of your body. The Goddess is ready to dance with you. I know you can feel her, sense her and hear her calling. Let her bring you back home to your soul. The embodiment of her wisdom will set us free.

The Sacred Feminine is truly rising.

ABOUT THE AUTHOR

TANYA LEBLANC

Tanya has been travelling to India for over 25 years and has trained in both Flamenco and Classical Indian Dance. She is a socially conscious entrepreneur and the founder and owner of Love Not Fear Inc, a conscious lifestyle and fashion brand. She is also a children's book author, playwright, and director and is the creator of an interactive children's show called The Big Wind Series. She is a certified Hatha Yoga teacher, and specializes in Shakti Yoga and Yoga Nidra. She is also the creator of The Shakti Sadhana Oracle, a 54 card deck featuring 13 Goddesses with sacred practices and meditations. Tanya is a Moon Dancer with Danza de la Luna in Mexico City and travels each year between Mexico, Canada, and India. Tanya is honoured to be part of *We are the Sacred Feminine Rising*.

Website: www.lovenotfear.ca
Instagram: @spread_lovenotfear
Instagram: @theshakti_collective

TANYETTE COLÓN

EMBOLDENED LIFE: BECOME THE ARTIST AND CREATOR OF YOUR LIFE'S CANVAS WHILE FLOWING INTO YOUR DHARMA

*"Great leaders **embolden** the rest of us to rise to our highest potentialities, to be active, insistent and resolute in affirming our own sense of things."*

- Arthur Meier Schlesinger Jr.

*L*ife is a never-ending kaleidoscope alchemizing the light and mirrors to reflect objects of beauty and a rainbow of fascinating patterns. These patterns are consistently changing and symbolize the human journey. There is a comfort in our predictability drenched in the mundane routines that are part of the foundation to maintain our existence, but as the kaleidoscope teaches us, the Universe does not move in a linear sense. Just when we become comfortable, a new mirror appears, and an invitation is presented with a choice to face it and grow or resist and repeat. If anything, the last year and a half has taught us life can change in a New York minute.

Humans have been telling stories since we have had the ability to speak. It is through the power of storytelling that humans can connect to the limitless layers of heart resonance. Storytelling can be a great catalyst for learning. During the early years of the Viking era, no poetry or sagas were written. Their stories were told in group settings. The men who memorized the stories were known as Viking Skalds, who were in charge of bringing these audible stories to life from generation to generation.

Our own story is a repository of memories and experiences. Our triumphs and losses and, no matter how we decide to breathe life into our story's blueprint, each one of us has the ability to inspire others to step into their *Emboldened Voice* and, in turn, answer their individual call to be of service to the world.

"We delight in the beauty of the butterfly, but rarely admit the changes it has gone through to achieve that beauty." - Maya Angelou

For many years I played far too small. I convinced myself it was humble to be a wallflower and the back of the meeting room was a cozy space to call home. My voice would quiver when I would speak up at a meeting. Oh, and then there were the voices. The cast of characters trying to take the leading role. It felt daunting at times to navigate a noisy mind of conditioned narratives. It's not to say I wasn't successful. I was in the top 10 percent at my corporate job, managing a seven-figure book of business. I had made some early career choices that had me in the public eye, but somehow I had reached some level of mastery to remain hiding behind a false mask whose couture label would read "good girl" in order to please societal expectations and to make people feel comfortable with my presence in a room. By the time I was in my late 30's, I felt numb inside, as if I had lost the complete essence of who I was until I started to get debilitated with the idea of trying to be perfect and slowly started to embark on an inner journey back to the remembering of my totality.

If you are reading this and are feeling fatigued from playing small in your daily life and have heard a whisper coming from deep within to finally step into your power—I See You because I AM You, and there has never been a more important time to rise as a collective for the greater good of humanity.

2020 was the deepest journey that I have ever taken to the darkest echo chambers within. To feel is a gift. Without an open heart, there is no gateway to the kingdom that is your inner garden where all of your divine intelligence resides. I have chosen to share some of these delicately weaved micro-moments in time in hopes that a phrase, a word, or a scene provides you with a skeleton key that will unlock a portal of undeniable force within you, so you no longer hide from your shine, and unleash the dazzling fire within.

JANUARY 2020—HAZY SHADE OF WINTER

" I hope she'll be a fool-- that's the best thing a girl can be in this world, a beautiful little fool." - F. Scott Fitzgerald

When the clock struck 2020, I was dancing my way into the new year in Oslo, Norway, at a 1920s Gatsby soiree with a glass of champagne in hand, which is appropriate because my vintage soul sings for anything from that era. I've always had an immersed connection with the book "The Great Gatsby". Jay Gatsby had a dreamer's quality about him, which resonated with me at a young age. I grew up on the poverty line and always found myself daydreaming into the possibilities life offered, and I was determined to rewrite the socio-economic script for myself.

The 1920s had as much hope and possibilities as 2020 did. Most people don't know that this era brought the birth of the "New World Transformers". There was a new kind of entrepreneur entering into the rise of capitalism. They mostly came from immigrant families, humble beginnings and viewed the world outside of the proverbial box. A world of innovation would begin, and the shift could be felt across the globe.

The idea of entering 2020, a new decade, brought a reprise of 1920's references and home interior design on social media, the news, and trendy magazines. Much like the Great Gatsby, we saw a merging of old world meets new world. As a Gen X woman, I also understood that the last time my generational archetype made an appearance was in the late 1800s-1930s with the likes of Thomas Edison and Nikola Tesla. The **Sacred Feminine** art deco queen of that time was embodied by Margaret Bourke-White, who shattered glass ceilings by being the first female photojournalist for Life magazine. She also rented the penthouse level of the Chrysler building from Walter Chrysler, which is how she captured one of her most iconic pictures. She once stated, "Photography found me." There was more historical significance between the two eras than the feather headpieces and sequin adorned dresses would have us believe.

Even with all of this promise, there was something deep inside of me that felt like a massive wave of change was coming as we transitioned into this new decade. There was a late winter storm brewing, and it would forever change the world as we know it......

FEBRUARY 2020—AN EVENING OF MAGIC AND THE COPPER CHALICE

*"The purpose of life is to live it, to taste experience to the utmost, to reach out eagerly and without fear for newer and richer experiences." - **Eleanor Roosevelt***

Time is the supreme magician—the wise crone morphing into sand encapsulated in an hourglass.

A dimension where a minute can feel like forever, and a lifetime of memories can flash by in a minute. It doesn't matter what scientific theory you subscribe to—*time* is the ultimate illusion. This moment —the very moment you read this—is the only absolute. Now is the only guarantee we have. What does it mean to be in the now in a world where ego and anxiety are in overdrive? Where a bevy of distractions like social media numbs us from feeling, and we deny ourselves connection to the very things that matter. The now gives us exotic brushstrokes of time that can never be repeated but as a collective create a canvas of texture, vibrancy and a well-lived life.

This was the elixir I devoured and co-created from for the second half of 2019. In many ways, I had started to manifest the foundation of what I had been dreaming of: I was living in both New York City and Oslo, Norway. My healthcare tech start-up had just taken flight into the market, and in the late summer of 2019, the Universe also brought a chance meeting with a dapper gentleman I lovingly called the "Viking Italiano" because of our shared love of Italy. My inner-child was happily co-creating a world of adventure and play. I remember the first time I met Steinar for coffee—it activated what I can only describe as a soul's remembrance. As I walked up to the table, he had the biggest smile, and his aura just shined so brightly...I remember thinking, "This feels like home." What was supposed to be a one hour coffee chat slowly merged into vino and aperitivo time at a bewitching Italian restaurant just a few steps away. This was the beginning of some adventurous curated dates around Oslo, and I always loved how Steinar met me at that door of curiosity, even if it was out of his normal comfort zone. Looking back, it's one of the things I loved about him—for just a moment, he too surrendered into the now.

*"I dream of painting, and then I paint my dream..." - **Vincent Van Gogh***

Vincent Van Gogh was known for merging fantasy into reality. His art pieces were full of passion and symbolic colors that expressed emotions. He also loved the night sky because the stars were a catalyst for him to dream. In late February 2020, Steinar and I headed out for an evening of magic. We met for a glass of wine overlooking the harbor in Aker Brygge at sunset. The Italian restaurant felt like a glasshouse perched at tree level, which was perfect for capturing the beauty of Oslo's late winter sky robust in light blue and yellow hues. During dinner, we journeyed into one of our most profound conversations about our dreams and the life we looked forward to curating.

In our own way, we were like Van Gogh, painting outside the lines with vibrant colors bringing imagination and parts of our intuition into the 3D. Steinar lovingly looked at me from across the table and said, "I wish you could see what I am seeing. There's this canvas. It's your canvas. The canvas of your life. It is majestic—encompassing everything you have been dreaming of." There was a part of him that knew I was still hiding. Weeks would pass before his words would fully sink into the depths of my heart. I then looked at him and said, "The very thing you run away from is the place where all of your power as a human is stored—that gorgeous heart of yours—the essence of who you are. You have the gift to help others who struggle with Type 1 diabetes, and I can't wait to see how everything comes together on your journey in the coming months..." His eyes watered, and I knew a seed had been planted into his heart. In many ways, we were each other's mirror, seeing the reflection of our divine light within. He said other words to me that evening that became a series of skeleton keys that would help me unlock some doors within my inner garden during some of my darkest nights of the Covid 19 pandemic in NYC.

The evening ended with a magic show by a talented Oslo alchemist called Labib Malik and a toast to the moment with a special drink brought to me in a copper chalice. In ancient times, the chalice was a sacred vessel used to drink in ceremonial practice. It reminds us to find the sacred in these delicate moments. I often wonder if our higher selves knew something was coming.

I hugged him, and we said goodbye. Neither of us knew that this would be the last time we would see each other for some time. Much like Paulo Coelho's book The Alchemist, the Universe would send us on our individual journeys. One of my voyages would lead me to embracing unconditional love in a world that only relates to conditions.

APRIL 2020—WHEN THINGS ARE FALLING APART, THEY ARE ACTUALLY FALLING IN PLACE

An invisible freight train had made its way into the U.S. and, like wildfire, took hold of New York City. The energy became dense, and fear was activated. I found refuge in hearing the birds chirping in the morning, the awakening of spring, and witnessing the morning sunrise from my bedroom window. I believe many of us felt this would only last for a few weeks, but soon those weeks became months, our faith would be tested as we walked a repeated loop. Many souls would leave Earth, and in exchange, a trail of grief was left behind.

By mid-April, my start-up was on hold due to the shutdowns and mistakes I had made as a first-time founder. I had lost 75% of my income in my corporate day life, and communication with Steinar became less frequent. It brought me to the concept of **"otra vez"** which translates to 'once again'. Starting all over again can feel like standing on the precipitous cliffside of life. I decided to take what money I had in savings and invested in myself: I had intensive weekly sessions with my mentor, joined Aubrey Marcus's Fit for Service community, participated in women circles, nurtured my thirst for learning, and started experiencing various healing modalities. The one thing I was clear about is that I did not want to exit this moment in history the same way I entered. The fragility of life was clear, and I was answering the call within that was no longer a whisper.

My very first introduction to Shamanic breathwork was in late March of 2020 via a Zoom call. It was one of the keys left for me to navigate the collective choppy pandemic waters. Seventy percent of our body's toxins are released through the breath. Breathwork provided a cathartic release for me. In a poetic sense, we take our first breath on Earth when we are born. That rhythmic life force of air flow—we take it in—to have it light our inner being then out. It's almost effortless. Our breath grounds us on a stressful day, and like a well composed song for a film, it will accelerate with our joy or excitement. There were III people on that Saturday journey with me. We were a global community from different cultures and religious beliefs. We were united as one collective lung—breathing hope into the world.

"As I walk through the valley of the shadow of death, I will fear no evil: for you are with me...."— *Psalm 23*

Psalm 23 is the most popular of all the Psalms. It speaks of the divine source within us all and how we are never truly alone no matter what challenges we face. I held this verse close to my heart as I dove deeper into the unearthing of trauma I had buried deep inside of me. Breathwork would become one of my consistent practices to meet myself. It was through my breath that I met my pain, I was given visions, I met with my guides, and I felt unexplainable bliss. Each dance with pain brought in an eruption of wails that had gone ignored for far too long. I was in a continuous process of shining love and light to my inner-child, my unworthiness, sense of brokenness, body shaming, and the sexual abuse I had blocked out as a child but had carried on a cellular level for most of my adult life.

On a collective scale, our breath would symbolically mean more than we could ever comprehend in the months to come. Covid 19 would attack our very ability to breathe, the masks restricted our air flow, and the tragedy of George Floyd in May of 2020 would only compound our country's grief.

JUNE 2020—BEAUTY IS LOVE MANIFESTING IN FORM

"Grief expressed out loud, whether in or out of character, unchoreographed and honest, for someone we have lost, or a country or home we have lost, is in itself the greatest praise we could ever give them. Grief is praise because it is the natural way love honors what it misses.." **Martín Prechtel - author of The Smell of Rain on Dust**

When we think of grief, we automatically connect it to a death of a loved one, and it wasn't until a conversation with my dear soul sister Nici Graves in June of 2020 that I finally gave myself permission to fully immerse in the dance of grief. I had a biopsy on my left breast due to a lump that had appeared, my Norwegian uncle had just been diagnosed with Stage 4 cancer, communication stopped with Steinar, and I found myself on the journey of rebuilding my start-up platform from scratch. I was faced with my own mortality and that of the people I loved—the illusion of control became spotlighted—a thread had been pulled and a great unraveling occurred. I was on bended knee—everything was pointing to a complete surrender...

As humans, we meet loss on a daily—loss of love, loss of a job, loss of a dream, and loss of life as we know it. These losses sometimes can carry the weight of 100 mini deaths. Until Nici innocently gave me the invitation to make grief a friend, I had been carrying shame for having a couple of bad days. Despite doing the inner journey work, there was a part of me that wanted to fast track the cycle of healing—bypass, and get to the other side. I wanted to dust myself off and get back to work. This is what Western culture teaches us to do. It teaches us to mask up the illusion and feel less. And yet, we are a constellation of archetypes finding our way back home through the often chaotic yet beautifully messy thing we call life. As divine gardeners of our inner landscape, we learn that in order to expand our hearts, we must surrender to the rhapsody of life's symphony. We have to be willing to get messy and feel our way through all of it. We must meticulously tend to it. On the other side of this journey is an enormous amount of grace and compassion for ourselves that can then be poured into the world.

AWAKEN TO THE GNOSIS

Gnosis is the grand awakening of your authentic soul. You answered the call, moved past your life traumas and attachments to societal conditioning. You remember you were always whole—a boundless human who no longer accepts the repressed antiquated ideologies that define the masses. It's coronation time. You are **LOVE**, my Queens and Kings. This is where your ancestors and guides celebrate with bliss. You have found your way back home. This space is exhilarating, empowering, and peaceful. You realize—it was always you. You are the journey. Gnosis is the consciousness of your true nature, outside the conditioned limitations of time, space, and consensus reality. You have connected with the divine source within and now view the world in that same divinity. Your copper chalice runneth over.

This is the space where the Sacred Feminine rises—in the "gnowing" that there is nothing to search for. You gracefully rise to the totality of your being. It is in this space where I fastened my crown for the second half of 2020. I had already courageously walked through the shadow of the valley of death, and my rebirth was fueled by gnosis. I was ready to serve. I came out of hiding and started doing multiple interviews with everyday heroes on Instagram. My platform was clear: I was inspiring others to step into their authentic voices so they could be of service to their communities. I strategically looked at old dinosaur systems that were holding certain communities back and became an advisor for a start-up digital bank created exclusively to serve the historically underbanked and underserved. I joined the ambassador group of an incredible non-profit called The Allingment Chapter (http://www.theallignmentchapter.org/) founded by a fierce woman called Raynell Jones who has helped thousands of single mothers across the U.S. with boxes of essentials and financial literacy. I created my Emboldened Entrepreneur live summit series with a culturally diverse speaker panel to serve medicine to the courageous humans who felt called to join and helped women to reconnect to their heart-centered why so they could reignite their purpose. As my friend Claire Spencer once said, "People only need the invitation to step into their boldness..."

SO HERE IS MY INVITATION:

Are you courageous enough to walk through the labyrinth to meet all parts of yourself?

Can you let go of the need to fix yourself so you can arrive at the gates of oneness?

Can you hold compassion and grace for yourself so that you may step into the world and offer all of that love in return to others?

Can you view the people that you love for the delicious human totality of WHO they are?

FEEL ALL OF IT MY DARLINGS, THEN RISE...

Rise like Mary Magdalene, the Apostle of the Apostles.
Rise like Mother Mary and bring that sacred compassion into the world.
Rise like the Egyptian Goddess Isis, who represents death and rebirth.
Rise like Eir, The Norse Goddess of Healing.
Rise like Kali Ma, who is fierce, compassionate and fearless.

Because You are the **Sacred Feminine Rising.** I am the **Sacred Feminine Rising. WE are** the **Sacred Feminine Rising.** Now, get ready to share your unique voice with the rest of the world and be a change agent for the greater good of humanity.

As I write these final words, it is now June 2021. I am two weeks away from the relaunch of my tech start-up and about to release my business academy. I said adios to my corporate job and have embraced the full scope of my dharma. I wanted to take a moment to thank the amazing humans who walked the last fifteen months alongside me: my family, amazing friends, the Fit for Service community, my mentor Billie-Lue Fung, and my gorgeous teen son

Ambrose who is one of my greatest teachers. A special heartfelt thank you to Steinar, for inspiring me to see the beauty in all parts of me and for being the mirror that sparked this journey back to my Divine Queendom. I am now beginning to see the canvas you were speaking of on that evening back in February 2020.

To the sacred readers, thank you for holding space. May your heart's resonance be your beacon, and I look forward to following your **Emboldened Life.** Let's keep in touch <3.

Con Mucho Amor,
T-

ABOUT THE AUTHOR

TANYETTE COLÓN

Tanyette Colón is the founder of InFuuse, which is an omni-channel communication platform that is the digital door between marketing and where the customer journey begins. InFuuse humanizes a business by eliminating the usual lag time that exists with responding to new client contacts.

She is also the Founder of Emboldened Entrepreneur, which helps entrepreneurs and smbs to uncover latent revenue in their operations through proprietary software. She assists in humanizing their marketing strategies and approach to community outreach. Emboldened Entrepreneur customizes social cause based virtual events to help build awareness on topics like: Diversity & Inclusion, Mental Health, and more.

Tanyette is currently part of the advisory board for Paybby, a digital bank created exclusively to serve the historically underbanked and underserved. Paybby, powered by the Wicket Banking app, seeks to empower our customers by providing smarter banking, innovative tools to manage finances, and opportunities to break the cycle of poverty, recirculate funds, and build wealth within and for our communities.

Website: www.infuusehealth.com

Website: www.emboldenedentrepreneurs.com

Instagram: https://www.instagram.com/tanyette

LinkedIn: http://linkedin.com/in/tanyettecolon

VANESSA FERARRO

THE WEALTHY GODDESS MOVEMENT

"The Purpose of Life is to Serve" - Dr & Master Sha

*D*ear Beloved Soul,

I know there is a desire deep in your heart and Soul to create something bigger than yourself that ignites purpose, fulfillment, creativity and can simultaneously support you to thrive financially. The problem we face with this desire is the sincere question...

Is there a way for us to flourish financially and be soulfully aligned at the same time?

Or is it true that we must trade one for the other? Is the cost of wealth in this physical world at the cost of something else? Does wealth cost us our mental, emotional or physical health, our time, our morals, ethics, integrity, our kindness, our essence, our principles, and values?

Can we be soulfully aligned with Heaven while building wealth on earth?

As a woman who has created a multiple six-figure business, has nine incredible women on her team, supported hundreds of clients through my programs and private coaching containers, I still to this day am transforming my shame and guilt around money.

This is an ongoing process. Through this chapter, my commitment is to share with you the wisdom that has shifted me to new timelines and has supported me to dream bigger than I ever have before.

I wish to share with you deep wisdom that will acknowledge we are healing much more than just our childhood traumas or limiting beliefs. The work we are doing in our personal growth and the desire to serve through our business is karmic.

It is deeper than our current memories or hidden trauma. It goes all the way back to the root, all the way back to the SOUL.

The universal truths that govern this planet and our world seep into our reality through our thoughts, behaviors, speech and influence our creations, relationship, health, business, and our finances.

How to heal our inner dialogue and fear around having money, making more money, wanting more money and what we actually do with our money is an ongoing teaching that has been with us for lifetimes. Every lifetime, we are consistently revealing a new layer of where the wound hurts, where we can still do better and where there is more growth for us to experience.

With every dollar we make, every dollar we lose, and every dollar in between, we are exchanging information in the quantum field that is changing not just your life but all women around the world.

The more you make, the more you invest, the more you allow for the current of your currency to flow, the more healing is available to every woman. For you, for me, for all of us.

Imagine creating, launching, and scaling a business you have channelled from the Divine Realm that connects you not just to others but deepens and transforms your relationship to the Soul of

Money, the Soul of your Business, and the Soul of your clients all the while uplifting your Soul's Standing in the cosmos.

This is the realm I choose to live and operate in. This is what I teach my clients.

This is how I am able to THRIVE in these most uncertain times.

There are many healers and business coaches out there who are absolutely brilliant

(Truth is I've hired many of them) but what makes my teachings and programs different is the SOUL WISDOM AND POWER through the TAO as taught by my beloved teacher, Dr. & Master Zhi Gang Sha.

For this reason, I can confidently say that with an 18-year background in sales and marketing development combined with Tao Healing Technology, that the application of these teachings can support us to align to a whole new dimension of existence, the Soul of TIME.

Yes, beloveds, we are living prophetic times. This era we are birthing is known to many as the Soul Light Era, The New Earth, The Aquarian Age.

This is important for us to understand and for our Soul's to remember.

You are here to SERVE. This is your purpose. To make others happier, healthier, empowered, and enlightened.

As you commit to this service, to this purpose, Divine Flourishing occurs.

Money, in my experience, has been a by-product of my alignment to Source, to The Tao, to my Soul, and to my Heaven's Task and by offering sincere service.

I truly believe if you commit to this, you will prosper and you will flourish.

I know there is a part of you that feels completely capable and deserving and another part of you that is scared and feels deeply unworthy. What I want you to know more than anything is this is not a coincidence, and more importantly, it's not your fault. The current programs running our planet and taught to our mothers, and carried in our ancestral line, carries negative information, not all of it our own. WE may not be personally responsible for all of it, but we are responsible for transforming it.

For many of us, including myself, entrepreneurship wasn't this romantic idea that I would just love to experience because it'd be so much fun. It was out of survival that I needed this to work. This is sometimes where we start, this is where I started and there is nothing wrong with that. But it is not where we want to stay. It is not where we want to stand.

Because these vibrations are filled with fear, lack, scarcity, worry, judgement, anger, pain, and more. We must remember the vibrations we operate in are more important than the acts themselves. It is our sole responsibility to uplift our vibration as much as possible, and when moving through dark crevices of our own psyche and heart, to bring compassion and forgiveness to all of it.

It's fascinating to me that even after creating a multiple six-figure business through very challenging times, serving others wholeheartedly, breaking through money trauma, and more, I still experience shame and guilt when it comes to earning and receiving more money.

This only makes sense to me as I began the road of understanding the teachings of Karma.

Karma is a heavy subject for many, and for many years I thought it was some moral compass that I could not understand.

Thankfully, a book called Tao Science written by Dr. Sha alongside Quantum Physicist Dr. Rulin Xiu, I am able to share with you a very simple and scientific explanation for deep spiritual teaching.

"What is Karma?

Karma is the record of services.

Karma is the information, energy, and matter carried by our vibrational field about the past services offered by our ancestors and ourselves.

Karma is recorded within the vibrational field. Our vibrational field records all of our actions, behaviours, and thoughts from the beginning of our existence. " - Tao Science

When we begin to transform the negative information in our field, in our body, cells, and cell units, it transforms all the way to the DNA and RNA level.

Imagine, even the spaces in between our cells, our connection to others through quantum entanglement begins to reverberate through the cosmos, and the repercussions of these changes, subtly and in not so subtle effects are felt.

This is what ancestral, generational, personal, and collective healing is.

To grasp a picture of this, I will share a woman's story who has deeply impacted my life.

I would love to introduce you to Teresa Leon Paredes.

Teresa Leon Paredes was born in Valparaiso, Chile, on March 4th, 1941

The oldest of four children. Her father, a baker, her mother a housewife.

I wish I could tell you of the happiest of childhoods, and although I can only pray there were moments of joy, I don't know many of those stories, but I do know this of her life.

At eight years old, Teresa's mother got very sick. Teresa was taken out of school and her studies to learn how to care for her three younger brothers and sister. Her time learning how to read was traded with learning how to take over her mother's role as the caregiver in the house.

When Teresa's mother died, she had very little time to mourn her as she became very busy cooking three meals a day, cleaning the house, knitting and sewing their clothes, and escorting her siblings to the school that she used to attend.

I cannot even fathom the thought that this was the world of a young nine years old girl.

At the age of fourteen, she married a man ten years her senior.

He was a kind, soft, very tall, dark, and handsome marine.

He came from a decent family, which at that time meant he wasn't abusive, nor was he an alcoholic. He loved her instantly and chose her to be his wife.

Within a year, she had her first child.

By the age of 29, Teresa had experienced nine pregnancies.

One miscarried. One was stillborn. And seven were healthy children.

Four girls and three boys. By the time Theresa was 30 years old, she had spent more than half her life taking care of others. Less than three years later, her country was torn apart in a military coup that killed her president, his family, all his constituents and made her, her husband, and her seven kids a moving target for the new regime that was taking over the country.

Her husband went missing, and she was forced to raise her kids in deep fear with very little resources, unsure of how she was to survive. Nine months later, with missing fingers, deep wounds, and bruises all over his body, her husband returned home only to tell her, "you must hide, you must take the children, and you must go."

It was not safe for him to travel with them, so they concocted a plan to meet in Argentina.

It was then that Theresa took her seven children with anything they could fit in their knapsack and fled Valparaiso, Chile, in hopes of living a new life in a new country in peace and harmony. Many terrible things happened along the way, but they did make it.

They lived in a refugee camp in Argentina until Canada announced that they would welcome 25,000 Chilean Families to Ontario, Canada.

This was one of the biggest blessings of Teresa's life.

Once again, she had very limited resources but felt incredibly wealthy for the very first time.

"Tus tres territorios
De cultura pura... tu belleza
de grandenza infinita
Mezcla de razas
Collar solemne de copihues *
entrelazados rojos y blancos.
Escrito Mayo 1989
 Teresa Leon, Poet
Poesia Errante 1993

The story of Teresa is that of my grandmother and of women all over the world.

We all have a grandmother or great grandmother who has been defined by the role she plays as a caregiver to others around her. It's what we are taught, it is what we learn, even if not consciously, it's what our ancestral lineage and its information that is felt within us.

An example of this comes to mind when I began renting a fabulous condo downtown and invited my mother to live with me. I remember the first night she stayed, how uncomfortable she was. "This building is too fancy," she would say. "Everyone is rich here," She would say. She felt we didn't belong like we didn't fit, and instead of enjoying the expansion of our quality of life, my mother contracted... and I could feel all of it.

I recall sitting her down and saying with as much kindness as I could, "Mom, I really need you to get on board with this. I am going to launch the next level of my business in this condo, and I can't be held back. I need your support but will do it without you if I have to.

Either, please, get aligned with what I am up to, or we can look for another place to have you be more comfortable... but I can't be around this energy. I have to do this. Are you in, or are you out? "

My mother cried tears of acknowledgement. She hugged me. She got it. She saw what I was committed to creating, and she knew she wanted to support me on the way.

Which is exactly what she did.

She cooked for me often, she cleaned the house, she made sure I went for walks, and she would silently sneak in my tea and coffee throughout the day. I appreciated all of it. I felt so supported and loved by her. She made a huge difference in the quality of my life and my experience as I broke through some limits and had the biggest month of sales in my business to date at the time.

You see, when you choose to become the woman you want to be, and that woman is wealthy in a lineage of women who weren't, you become the first to transform this ancestral karma. The guilt and shame we feel most times is not our own, and it always seems to be in the shadows, right on the other side of celebration and joy.

This is an example of having both positive and negative information in our field.

As I have begun to surpass new levels, scaling my services and my wealth, I am discovering for myself that when I hide celebrating the results The Source has blessed me with, I am hiding the many blessings available to others in choosing what I have chosen.

Purpose, Service, Surrender, Trust, Generosity, Kindness, Love, Devotion, and obedience to that which cannot be named.

"The ego loves to take credit for God's work."

When I do not celebrate "the wins" because of my ancestral or personal karma, I rob myself the opportunity to celebrate the Divine - for it is the virtue of heaven that blesses my life - not my own drive and strong will because the truth is, it's not me, it has never been, and that is a blessing.

My willingness to open my heart, to anchor my Soul's work, and show up every day, even when I don't feel like it, especially when I don't feel like it is what has paid off the most.

It is no longer survival that feeds me to act, but rather, alignment to my purpose and heaven that carries me through. Heaven is doing most of the work, we just need to show up to do our part.

Survival instincts have existed in our ancestors and us for millennia.

Knowing this, it creates an easier path to forgive the negative feelings and emotions that come up when we intentionally align to creating more wealth in our lives. What I am starting to understand for myself is the shame that I still hold as a wealthy woman ties into the lineage of my grandmother, Teresa Leon Paredes.

This is what I am transforming in my practice, with every meditation, every time I chant, every time I pray and bow to my altar. I am at the service of the Divine, and I ask for guidance for every step of the way. I no longer wish to operate from a place of survival but from a place of thriving in my Soul power.

"Knowledge lasts for decades, Wisdom lasts for eons." - Dr. & Master Zhi Gang Sha

There's so much that I have yet to discover about my own feminine aspects and Soul Power as I study books and listen to teachers talking about masculine and feminine polarities and energies and the spectrum in between.

> However, I have found some peace in the teachings of Dr. & Master Zhi Gang Sha.

The Tao Teachings channelling through Dr. & Master Sha simplify a very convoluted conversation. They bring clear and fundamental teachings that are universal and can be found governing our body, our blood, our internal systems, tissues, muscles, and bones.

This wisdom also includes Mother Earth, all stars, all planets and galaxies, and beyond.

This Universal teaching is simple; and can be found in almost any of his 22 books, 11 New York Times Best Sellers.

Master Sha teaches that everyone and everything is made up of SHEN (Soul, heart, mind), Qi(energy), and JING (matter)

Soul is the content of the information in everyone and everything.

Heart includes the physical heart and spiritual heart.

The spiritual heart is the receiver of the information in everyone and everything.

Mind is the processor of the information in everyone and everything.

Energy is the ability to do the work, such as lifting a weight.

Energy is the actionar of everyone and everything.

Matter is the physical reality.

It is everything we can measure: weight, length, height, charge, mass, electrical field, shape, color, frequency, and other physical properties and quantities. **Matter is the transformer of everyone and everything.**

As quoted in book Tao Science, co authored alongside Quantum Physicist Dr. Rulin Xiu, the manifestation process is :

SOUL> HEART> MIND> ENERGY> MATTER

This is true ALIGNMENT.

For many years we have been using the mind to direct the energy and actions we take and "manifest" things, but you cannot heal or manifest through the mind alone. Mind over matter is not enough. Soul OVER MATTER is where it's at.

Transforming your mind and the quality of the vibrational frequencies and thought patterns you hold allow you to tap into a new current of information.

When this information is aligned and channelled through your heart from your SOUL, this is POWER.

It is also important to note it is not only us who are made up of Shen, Chi, Jing but also our parents, our families, our businesses, our relationships, our clients, and yes, even our money. Money has a SOUL. Your Business has a SOUL. Your relationship with your Business is a SOUL!

It's all information, personal, generational, and collective.

Layers of it that include the history of all women across all time and space.

This is what we are transforming.

This is what The Wealthy Goddess Movement is about.

Yes, as a company, we stand for wealth advocacy for women and financial education.

However, emotional, mental and spiritual healing is the foundation.

We stand for healing at the SOUL level, to transform the negative information in all our fields to one of LOVE, PEACE & HARMONY and SERVICE.

When we begin to operate our business and service through love, forgiveness, compassion, light, humility, and harmony, we in turn FLOURISH.

If we do not share this flourishing with gratitude in our heart, service in our minds, and bring enlightenment to ALL SOULS, we lose.

Notice the words I used there carefully. If we do not SHARE this flourishing with others... we lose.

CURRENCY is a CURRENT of energy.

Money is a current, and it wants to flow.

Flow into your life and the lives of others, serving us all to uplift the quality of life for ourselves, our families, and all those around us. When we begin to understand these universal laws and how they exist in all things, we are being invited to see things from a quantum level, from a SOUL Level.

We align to the support from Heaven to flourish on Mother Earth, all the while uplifting our Soul Standing in the cosmos.

This is how we manifest prosperity, abundance, and flourishing on Mother Earth while being deeply connected to Heaven.

It is possible. It's already happening. And it can happen for you.

" Heal the Soul first, and everything else will follow" - Dr & Master Zhi Gang Sha

The Sacred Feminine Rising is rising in all of us, men and women alike.

For each of us, it is purifying and manifesting different realities, all in hopes we will align.

That we may align to not only a higher purpose but to a more loving and peaceful experience as we fulfill that purpose.

My business has been my greatest love.

It was the Soul of my business that asked me to RISE into my leadership, into my power, into my service, and into my practice. As I scale my service and business, it requires more spiritual dedication and nourishment. The success of my business is a reflection of the success my Soul is experiencing in the Soul World. It goes together hand in hand, asking for me to open my heart further, love stronger, forgive faster, and serve unconditionally.

The Soul of my clients keeps me accountable, keeps me in service, keeps me in alignment, and brings me so much joy. The women I meet, that I speak to, the stories I get to hear, the space that is being held, and the transformation I get to witness are nothing short of miraculous. It is one of the most incredible blessings in my life.

And the money, the Soul of Money, is teaching me, each and every day, how to honor it more, how to serve with it more, how to establish new patterns of trust, integrity, justice, and peace. My business is a love story that has transformed my Soul.

"Ancestors plant the trees, descendants enjoy the shade" - Tao Science

What we commit to now will transform the path for all women after us.

This is the power we hold. This is the power of the US.

This is what is made possible when we claim our divine birthright and Soul's Power and embody the Wealthy Goddess Within.

ABOUT THE AUTHOR

VANESSA FERARRO

Vanessa Ferraro is a Leading Certified Tao Hands Practitioner, 6-Figure Soul-Based Business Strategist, CEO of The Wealthy Goddess Immersion, and Wealth Advocate for Women. Featured on spiritual networks like RA MA TV, Vanessa bridges strategy with spirituality to lead a new paradigm of business—one that empowers women with the soul, systems, and skills they need to serve more people and make a greater impact in the world.

Websites:
www.wealthygoddessmovement.com
www.nextleveltao.com
Instagram: www.instagram.com/wealthygoddessmovement

ABOUT SOULFULLY ALIGNED PUBLISHING HOUSE

Soulfully Aligned Publishing House exists to bring healing, transformation and aligned service through the written word to the world.

Created and founded by Best Selling Author, Sandra Rodriguez Bicknell and Vanessa Ferraro, their mission is to highlight the voices of healers around the world to the mainstream to exemplify the power of having a story, and not being your story. Soulfully Aligned Publishing donates all book proceeds to various charities around the world as chosen by their authors. We are committed to bringing conscious, harmonious principles to the way we operate our business and are here to magnify and empower all whom we work with to align to their Soul, their message and their service to the world.

Made in the USA
Monee, IL
24 November 2021